Simply
Packaging

To capture the ever-evolving art of packaging design and
reveal its reflection of the times

SimplySeries™
SimplyPackaging

First published and distributed by
viction:workshop ltd.

viction:ary™

Unit C, 7th Floor, Seabright Plaza, 9-23 Shell Street,
North Point, Hong Kong
URL: www.victionary.com
Email: we@victionary.com

Edited and produced by viction:workshop ltd.

Concepts & art direction by Victor Cheung
Book design by Cherie Yip @ viction:workshop ltd.
Cover images by Stockholm Design Lab
Preface by Shirley Surya

EUR & US edition
Printed and bound in China

content
contenido
inhoud
目録
コンテンツ
목차

preface
prefacio
voorwoord
前言
はしがき
서론

After two titles under Amatterofdesign™ series, Viction:ary presents yet another tome as part of the SimplySeries™ to attest to the no lack of exemplary packaging. The ubiquitous pack – canned, wrapped, boxed, tied, bottled, or clothed – is ever-present in our physical, visual and mental landscapes. Whether it is human insecurity to protect or sell, or the nobler purposes to communicate or intrigue, our container culture has been the medium and the message of both pragmatic and creative goals. Designers, like creative sponges, have learned to soak up and manipulate all different influences – artistic, cultural, lifestyle, political or technological – to create entirely fresh packaging designs that transcend mere cosmetic solutions. This book is thus well justified to capture the ever-evolving art of packaging design and its reflection of the times. Going beyond a focus on the visual impact, material and design concept that were presented in the Amatterofdesign™ series, this book looks at the entirety of each packaging design. From the realm of food and beverage, lifestyle and branding, projects will again demonstrate how modern day packaging has become one of the most sophisticated, holistic and powerful examples of the designer's craft.

But even with its ever-changing nature, packaging remains, for the most part, a manifestation of brand differentiation to trigger buys at the point of purchase. Branding and sales will continue to influence the form and function of packaging especially in a competitive commercial world, marked with what John Berger calls 'density of visual messages,' where products clamber for attention and where incredibly discerning consumers spend no more than a few seconds to pick a product off the shelf. Complexity in packaging design, therefore no longer consists of solving only functional or ergonomic aspects, or communicating all that the packaging contains or the benefits the product offers. The pack is no longer a passive sales canvas, but an active tool making its presence felt in the crowd. Communication clarity of the pack must now drive an emotional point of difference in addition to a rational one. The beauty and poetic elements of the designed object are some of the factors that will create a nexus between the product and the user.

In the chapter Gobbling Desires that presents selected food and beverage packaging, the combination of shape, colour, finish, material, typography, logo, and other surface graphics become a transfer of values, emotions or cultural codes that entice users to purchase and consume. While BVD's use of bright colours and playful type on the paper bag makes Candyking more appealing to children (P.165), Creative Method's design for the fast food to-go wrapping in fresh yellow, contrasted with grey scale photography of a streetside stall, makes the takeaway Mexican cuisine from Guzman Y Gomez seems just as authentic as having it served on the streets of Mexico City (P.200). By employing exquisite materials and genre-breaking structural design, Japanese design guru Kenya Hara reinvents the look of the traditional sake with his tall and slender Hakkin Sake bottles, made of reflective mirror-like surface that seems to make the bottles disappear in their environment (P.210). Similarly, the futuristic Nikka Whiskey bottles by acclaimed product designer Michael Young are far from what we would instinctively expect whiskey bottles to look alike, making the good ol' beverage appeal to a whole new generation (P.170). Inspired by the beekeepers, New York-based Little Fury's design of clear frame-like honey containers within a wooden case is a contemporary way of displaying the varying colours and quality of different honey without losing the familiar touch (P.171). From the shape, tactile elements, lexical and visual languages, sometimes even the sound, the pack communicates lifestyle aspirations on a subliminal level as it provokes astonishment, surprise or fascination. These combined elements become more significant as the pack becomes something to value in its own right – an object of display and status badge at home or at work.

As the living embodiment of a brand's value and personality, packaging design is stretched even further in today's complex market scenario. To move through the chaos and state of entropy, it is obliged to take up innovative methods, processes and concepts, towards either massive personalisation, diversification in the uniformity, even ambiguity or non-branding. Selected projects in the chapter Brand Seduction show how the goal of packaging design is going beyond sales, toward building an experience of 'touchpoints' between the user and the product or service. Tokyo Bar's Tokyo pop culture-inspired coasters and interiors by Samurai Inc (P. 56) and, fashion label Humor's overall identity design present on its t-shirts, shoe boxes, shopping bags and stickers by Bluemark Inc (P. 66), exemplify the value of packaging in molding immersive brand and user experience.

Representing the extreme of attitudinal packaging that works harder than simply acting as a mark of recall is Dutch design duo FormaFantasma's Colonna (P. 14). Composed of a necklace made of bone china porcelain, a horsehair tail and a book-coffer divided into four chapters, Colonna questions the state of luxury and sustainability in design by raising the ethical issue of using a horse's hair to make an accessory, for the sake of reusing every bit of an animal. This one-off project is an example of the quirky packaging-cum-product design that sells nothing but its own unspoken 'brand' – a design firm with its signature iconographical approach. It represents the capacity of today's use of packaging design for the purpose of seduction or comic evocation to make one gasp, think, smile, talk and not just buy.

While the craft and shock doctrine are largely utilised in packaging design to enhance product perception or brand equity, the rise of the savvy shoppers and their demanding criteria, including that of social responsibility, is bringing about a shift in the priorities of packaging design. Consumers are learning to choose a product that is more thoughtfully produced and those that embody the best aspects of green design. Not just about recyclability, today's consumers want to know the product's cradle-to-grave environmental impact – from where it is sourced to its reuse or disposal issues. Far from leading to the death in the art of packaging, this calls for a finer craft that achieves maximum seduction capacity, with the minimum material and energy consumption.

In the chapter Lifestyle Stimuli, which presents most of the book's eco-conscious packaging examples, Stockholm Design Lab's packaging and identity design for the office supply distributor, Askul may not be the most radical example in applying the 'green' aspiration (P. 90). But its simplicity and poetic use of Swiss-like typography, minimal use of graphics and material demonstrates how the fine art of packaging can elevate the status of the seemingly mundane everyday products. The green agenda is perhaps most evident in the overall idea and design of the Take-Out Garden by Korean design collective NoName NoShop (P. 126). These are specially designed biodegradable paper cups of soil planted with seeds distributed to encourage people to nurture the plants before transplanting them to green the rest of their neighbourhood. Knoend's Lite2go – a multi-functional, low-cost and lightweight lamp whose packaging becomes the shade for the light bulb – embodies smart packaging that marries good design and sustainability (P. 134). As one of the solutions to current backlash against over-packaged products in the shift towards less conspicuous consumption, Lite2go earned a Bronze in the 2008 International Design Excellence Award. While eco-conscious packaging is a virtue, it is perhaps perfected if coupled with design for user comfort. Help Remedies by Little Fury and Chapps Malina – a new line of environmental-friendly and design-savvy medical products – is one of such products. Not only is it packaged in 100% recycled compostable paper pulp, its modern design with a copy like 'Help. I have a headache.' set in sleek typeface, makes the fear-mongering pharmaceutical product category friendlier and more accessible to users (P. 122).

From packaging's determinant role in the brand infrastructure of products and services, to its shift toward socio-environmental consciousness, Viction:ary hopes the innovative solutions in this book be catalysts for better packaging ideas. In a highly competitive market, doubled with consumer skepticism, the means (and gimmicks) to impress through packaging design can be extreme and endless. But perhaps what we need more of, or what will truly rise above the flood, are honest packaging design that appeals to the eye, mind and heart, while being relevant to both the consumer and client – all while using the least for maximum impact.

brand seduction
de merk-verleiding
seducción de marca
品牌的誘惑
ブランド×誘惑
브랜드 유혹

Sometimes the best things are not for sale. Sometimes building a lasting impact counts more than one-off buys. Demonstrating how various forms of packaging well present a limited edition collector's item, or a bar or boutique's entire identity system, this chapter reveals the evident value of packaging in crafting immersive brand and user experience of products and services.

Ash Spurr
Derbyshire, UK

Title
* MTV Packaging Concepts ** Hex Clock

Client
* D&AD Brief
** Ash Spurr (Self-initiated project)

Art Director
* Ash Spurr
** Ash Spurr, Matt Keers, Adam Robson

Designer
* Ash Spurr
** Ash Spurr, Matt Keers, Adam Robson

Year Produced
* 2008 ** 2007

Description
* Initiated by D&AD, students were asked to interpret MTV as a virus. Knowing that the majority would go for a screen-based solution, Spurr decided to make it print-based instead.

A series of posters featuring the safety net medicine box packaging produced to be giveaways was designed to promote different MTV channels. The boxes were planned to be placed in shops, bars, and cinemas, etc.

** The Hex Clock is a screensaver clock whilst it is also a colour chart for web designers. The clock comes in card packaging, which encourages users to interact with its calendar-like doors and reveals the featured colours.

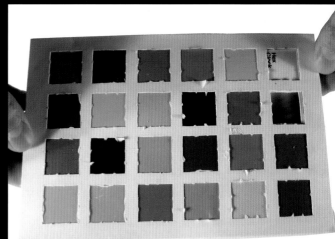

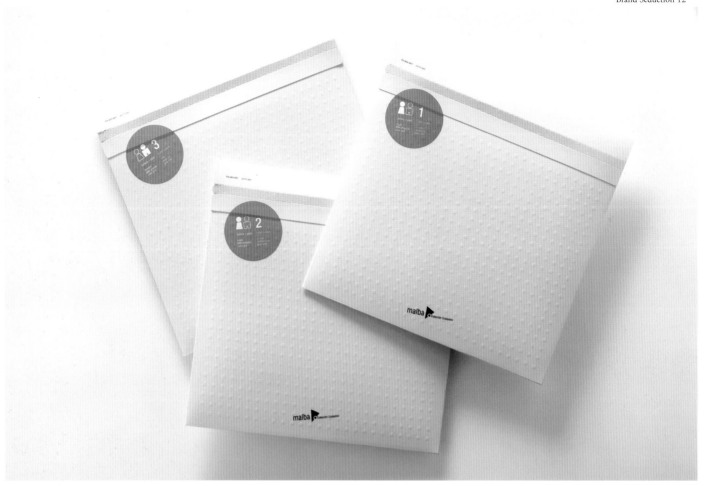

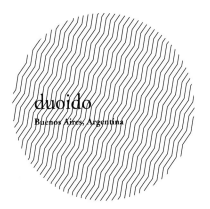

duoido
Buenos Aires, Argentina

Title
ArtPack

Client
Museum of Latin American Art, Buenos
Aires (MALBA)

Art Director
Luciana Echevarría, Diego López

Designer
Luciana Echevarría, Diego López

Year Produced
2006

Description
MALBA wanted to make their basic
products like the institutional t-shirt of the
museum, looks representative, long-lasting
and attractive. These products are displayed
and sold in MALBA store located at the
museum's lobby. The designers explored
the products' packaging under the strict
graphical and conceptual directions of the
brand identity.

The idea of a vinyl disc, that can be shown
as a painting, determined its approval. The
colour of sober trowel, the selection of
elements, and the crossing of textures differentiate the products and make them stand
out from the crowd.

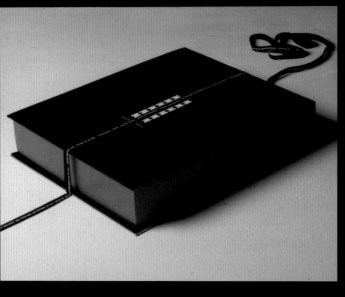

FormaFantasma.
Eindhoven, The Netherlands

Title
COLONNA

Client
FormaFantasma

Art Director
Andrea Trimarchi, Simone Farresin

Designer
Andrea Trimarchi, Simone Farresin

Year Produced
2007

Description
Producing an object can take up a lot of materials and energy. However, industrial rules for production and the idea of sustainability suggest us that, the fewer the materials the better.

FormaFantasma defines sustainability as the last expression of luxury and thus they design jewels accordingly to this. COLONNA represents their ancestral necessity to produce goods without a specific or more 'primal need,' so they used a valuable material, the entire horsehair tail, to raise the necklace to an iconic level as a metaphor of luxury.

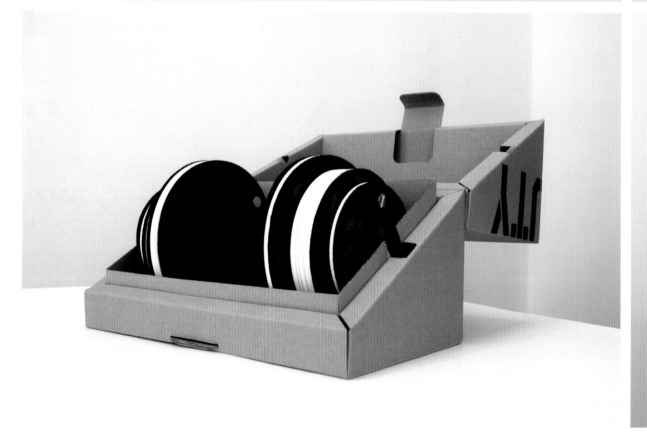

CoDesign Ltd
Hong Kong, China

Title
Heavy Duty

Client
Heiwa Paper Hong Kong

Art Director
Eddy Yu, Hung Lam

Designer
PakSum Leung

Year Produced
2008

Description
Heiwa Paper would like to produce a paper sample for their entire collection of heavy-weight papers.

CoDesign believes that it is important to impress people by the design itself rather than its graphic elements. What brings people beyond is the experience of using it. The designers eventually adopted the form of a dumbbell to convey the theme of the paper sample.

Title
Espluga Pack - Self Promotion

Client
espluga+associates

Art Director
espluga+associates

Designer
espluga+associates

Year Produced
2008

Description
Self-promotion packaging specially produced for espluga+associates lecture at a Packaging Conference in Barcelona, 2008.

Purpose Ltd
London, UK

Title
Panettone

Client
Greenford Printers

Art Director
Rob Howsam, Stuart Youngs

Designer
Charlotte Cline

Year Produced
2007

Description
Newly-established printer Greenford Print-ing wanted a memorable way to promote their business and at the same time wish their valued clients a 'Merry Christmas and Happy New Year' at their first Christmas.

By building on the familiar language of colour specification, Pantone swatches initi-ated the main theme for Purpose's concept. 'Panettone' created a colourful twist on the traditional Italian Christmas cake.

The Panettone boxes arrive as a set of 5, featuring special dates from Christmas Eve to New Years Day, each with a different pantone colour.

PANETTONE®
261207C

PANETTONE®
241207C

PANETTONE®
311207C

PANETTONE®
251207C

3KG
Hokkaido, Japan

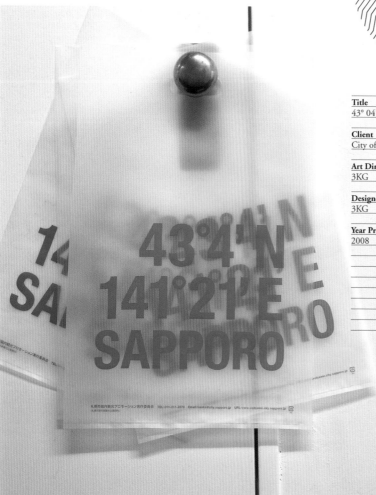

Title
43° 04' N & 141° 21' E

Client
City of Sapporo

Art Director
3KG

Designer
3KG

Year Produced
2008

Description
3KG were commissioned by City of Sapporo to renew their paper and plastic bags. Previous design was conservative and made from photos of tourist spots in Sapporo. 3KG decided to eliminate them all and designed the new bags from the ground. Making them functional both domestically and internationally was one of the main attention. Knowing that th city's information could give users some pictures of Sapporo even there is no actual images printed, only the latitude and longitude of the city centre was printed on the surface of bags. Two colours, pink and green, are available.

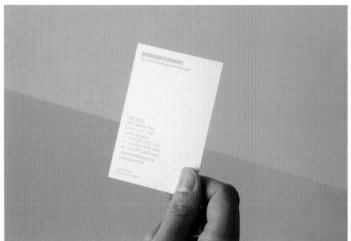
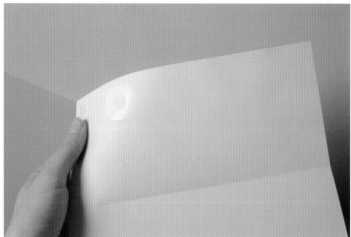

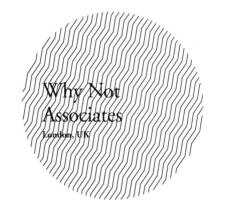

Why Not
Associates
London, U.K.

Title
The Reel

Client
The Reel

Art Director
Why Not Associates

Designer
Why Not Associates

Year Produced
2006

Description
Part of the re-branding exercise for a
subscription-based media resource company
The Reel, Why Not Associates designed the
packaging of their monthly-issued DVD
accompanied with a booklet. The designers developed a roll-fold pack around the
booklet with a clever sequence of folds that,
combined with a cut, holds the DVD in
place without using adhesives.

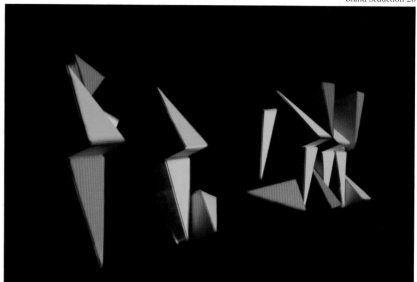

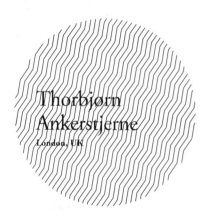

Thorbjørn
Ankerstjerne
London, UK

Title
Pflum Form

Client
Karsten Pflum

Art Director
Thorbjørn Ankerstjerne

Designer
Thorbjørn Ankerstjerne

Year Produced
2007

Description
Pflum Form is a modular typeface designed for live events, e.g. concerts and installations. Each letter consists of 3 to 8 triangular modules in three different heights. During a performance, the modules are illuminated by animated colours from a video projector. Since the projection is closely adjusted to hit only the triangles, it gives the impression that the light is part of the surface.

PFLUM FORM is a typeface designed for live use on a stage. During a performance projected animations illuminates the 3 dimensional shapes, creating a futuristic architecture.
The starting point for the triangular typeface is the sawtooth waveform, the base of almost all typical synthesizer sounds.
3 different heights of triangles has been used to create more depth and give the feeling of a "musical" landscape.

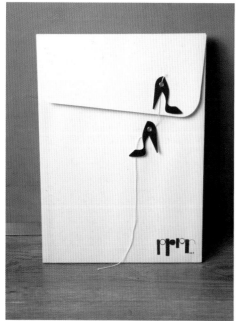

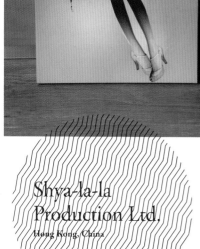

Shya-la-la
Production Ltd.
Hong Kong, China

Title
Pedder Red Spring/Summer 2007 Press Kit

Client
Pedder Group

Art Director
Benson

Designer
Benson

Year Produced
2006

Description
An interesting integrated packaging incorporating a premium giveaway, a corporate sales catalogue in CD format and press releases. Very user-friendly and as much a 'collectable' as the design-talking point.

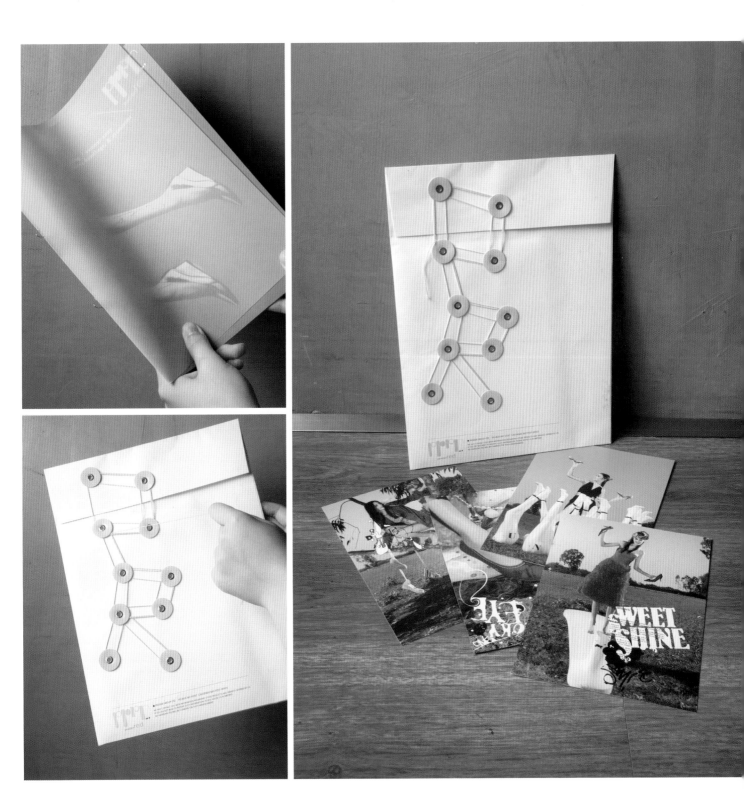

BaseDesign
Bruxelles, Belgium & New York, USA

Title
Se Vende Museo , Museum For Sale

Client
Carmen Cantón

Art Director
BaseDesign

Designer
BaseDesign

Year Produced
2007

Description
'Catalogue-piece "Museum For Sale," a mobile museum that materializes the Carmen Cantón Ego Art Center. The catalogue is presented in a box and reflects the artist's concept of translating her work into product.' By Ego Art Centre.

Title: Further Reductions
Ego Art Centre in Lima, Peru
Author: Carlos León-Xjimenez
Curated by: Jorge Villacorta
Location: Informal shopping center (in industrial ex-place) in Tacora's context (street market of objects in disuse and of the second hand) Cultural Centre of the Spanish Embassy in Lima,
Natalio Sánchez 181-185, Santa Beatriz, Lima, Peru
Date: 23/4/2003
09:00h - 14:45h
cleonxjimenez@gmail.com
www.geocities.com/carlosleon/

Title: Ego Art (Education) Centre
Ego Art Centre in Santo Domingo, Dominican Rep.
Author: Iliana Emilia
Curated by: Paula Gómez Jorge
Ubicación: Center of Spain Archbishop Meriño forma a corner(square) Archbishop With Freightages, Colonial City in Santo Domingo, Dominican Republic.
Date: 7/6/2003. 17:00h
mariflex@hotmail.com
www.losnoveles.net
Iliana Emilia-Centro de Arte Ego, 2003 - ...
iliana@ilianaemilia.net
www.tricom.net/cce

Title: Naturaleza Muerta
Ego Art Centre in Lima, Peru
Author: Maria Fe Nevares
Curated by: Jorge Villacorta
Location: Cultural Centre of the Spanish Embassy in Lima,
Natalio Sánchez 181-185, Santa Beatriz, Lima, Peru
Date: 22/4/2003
centrocultural@aeci.org.pe
mariflex@hotmail.com
www.caretas.com.pe

Title: f(l)oros.
Ego Art Centre in Lima, Peru
Author: José-Carlos Mariátegui
Curated by: Jorge Villacorta
Location: Cultural Centre of the Spanish Embassy in Lima,
Natalio Sánchez 181-185, Santa Beatriz, Lima, Peru
José Carlos Mariátegui Museum. Jr. Washington 1938-1946,
Lima I (Cercado)
Date: 23/4/2003 - 17:00h
centrocultural@aeci.org.pe
jcm@rcp.net.pe
www.rcp.net.pe/MARIATEGUI

Title: Via Crucis (Way of the Cross)
Ego Art Centre in Lima, Peru
Author: Manuel Munive Maco
Curated by: Jorge Villacorta
Location : Cultural Centre of the Spanish Embassy in Lima, Natalio Sánchez 181-185, Santa Beatriz, Lima, Peru
Date: 7/4/ 2003. 19.00 to 20:30 h
centrocultural@aeci.org.pe
www.urp.edu.pe

Title: Museum for sale
Author: Organization Ego Art Centre
Location: The Route of Sense, Gran Via 54, 28013 Madrid, Spain
Date: february 2005
Carmen Cantón-Ego Art Centre, 2000 - ...
LRS@larutadelsentido.org
www.larutadelsentido.org

Title: Five fingers inside (or five fingers in ego)
I. Museum-Ego Art Centre in the MARCO of Vigo, Spain
Author: Jorge Migoya
Curated by: Carmen Cantón
Location: MARCO - Museum of Contemporary Art of Vigo, Príncipe 54, 36202 Vigo, Pontevedra, Spain
Date: 17/12/2004 - 27/02/2005
Jorge Migoya-Ego Art Centre, 2005 - ...
jorgemigoya@hotmail.com
www.marcovigo.com

Title: Collectors Collect
I. Museu-Ego Art Centre in the MARCO - Museum of Contemporary Art of Vigo,
Author: Amaya González Reyes
Location: MARCO-Museum of Contemporary Art of Vigo, Príncipe, 54 36202 Vigo, Pontevedra, Spain
Date: 17/12/ 2004 - 27/02/2005
Amaya González-Ego Art Centre, 2005 - ...
amayagonzalezreyes@yahoo.es

Title: Signs of Identity
Ego Art Centre in Mexico City, Mexico
Author: Carmen Cantón
Localization: Cultural Office of the Spanish Embassy in Mexico City, Guatemala no 18, Centro Histórico, 06010 Mexico City., Mexico
Date: 3/10/2003
Carmen Cantón-Ego Art Centre, 2000 - ...
LRS@larutadelsentido.org
www.centrodearteespi.org

Title: Ego Art (Education) Centre
Ego Art Centre in Santo Domingo, Dominican Rep.
Author: Iliana Emilia
Ubicación: Center of Spain Archishop Meriño forms a corner(square) Archbishop With Freightages, Colonial City in Santo Domingo, Dominican Republic.
Date: 7/6/2003. 17:00h
Iliana Emilia-Centro de Arte Ego, 2003 - ...
iliana@ilianaemilia.net
www.tricom.net/cce

Title: Ego Art Centre in Venice
About Contemporary Spanish Art - Ophelia and Ulysses. Venice Biennais, Italy
Author: Carmen Cantón
Curated by: Rafael Doctor Roncero
Location: Pavilionof the Antichi Granei of the Giudecca. Venice, Italy.
Date: juny de 2001
Carmen Cantón-Ego Art Centre 2001 - ...
www.larutadelsentido.org

Title: Enrique Marty and I in Venice
Ego at the Küppersmühle Sammlung Grothe Museum, Duisburg, Germany
Author: Carmen Cantón
Curated by: Rafael Doctor
Location: Museum Küppersmühle Sammlung Grothe Philosophenweg 55, 47051 Duisburg, Germany
Date: On April 17 - May 16, 2001
kueppersmuehle_srt-online.de
www.museum-kueppersmuehle.de

Title: Museum Possible
Ego Art Centre in Lima, Peru
Author: Miguel Zegarra
Curated by: Jorge Villacorta
Location: Cultural Centre of the Spanish Embassy in Lima,
Natalio Sánchez 181-185, Santa Beatriz, Lima, Peru
Date: 23/4/2003 - 17:00h
mmzegarra@hotmail.com
www.artstudiomagazine.com
www.espacioft.com.ar

Title: Museum for sale
Locking Shocking
Author: Organization Ego Art Centre
Location: The Route of Sense, Gran Via 54, 28013 Madrid, Spain
Date: february 2005
kingshocking@lockingshocking.com
www.lockingshocking.com

Title: Museum Possible
Ego Art Centre in Lima, Peru
Author: Miguel Zegarra
Curated by: Jorge Villacorta
Location: Cultural Centre of the Spanish Embassy in Lima,
Natalio Sánchez 181-185, Santa Beatriz, Lima, Peru
Date: 23/4/2003 - 17.00h
mmzegarra@hotmail.com
www.artstudiomagazine.com
www.espacioft.com.ar

Title: Manuel Sánchez-Vergara
Ego Art Centre in Cordoba, Argentina
Authors: Soledad Sánchez y Carolina Vergara
Curated by: Luz Novillo Corvalán
Location: Spanish Cultural Centre in Cordoba, Entre Rios 40 - (5000) Cordoba, Argentina
Date: From June 26 until July 17, 2003
Soledad Sánchez-Ego Art Centre, 2003 - ...
ojoporojo@hotmail.com
info@ccec.org.ar

Title: Creating Forests
I. Museum-Ego Art Centre in the MARCO of Vigo, Spain
Author: Carlos Latorre
Curated by: Carmen Cantón
Location: MARCO - Museum of Contemporary Art of Vigo, Príncipe,54/ 36202 Vigo, Pontevedra, Spain
Date: 17/12/2004 - 27/02/2005
Carlos Latorre-Ego Art Centre, 2003 - ...
latorre53@hotmail.com
www.marcovigo.com

Title: Museum for sale
Author: Organization Ego Art Centre
Location: The Route of Sense, Gran Via 54, 28013 Madrid, Spain
Date: february 2005
Carmen Cantón-Ego Art Centre, 2000 - ...
LRS@larutadelsentido.org
www.larutadelsentido.org

Title: WOMD Weapons of Mass Destruction - attack luxurious hotel -
Ego Art Centre in Asuncion, Paraguay
Authors: Carmen Cantón y Fernando Moure
Curated by: Fernando Moure
Localization: Center of Visual Arts / Barro Museum, Street Grabadores del Cabichuy y Cañada, Ykuá Saty, Asuncion, Paraguay
Cultural Center of Spain Juan de Salazar, Tacuarí 745, Asuncion, Paraguay
Date: 29/5/2003
Fernando Moure-Ego Art Centre, 2003 - ...
fernandomoure@gmail.es
www.vivaparaguay.com

Title: ATLETICO ATTACKS THE EGO ART CENTRE!
Ego Art Centre in Mexico City, Mexico
Author: ATLETICO
Curated by: Ander Azpiri
Localization: Cultural Office of the Spanish Embassy in Mexico City, Guatemala no. 18, Centro Histórico, 06010 Mexico City, Mexico
Date: From October 9 to November 1, 2003
Balam Bartolomé-Ego Art Centre, 2003 - ...
cabezilapiz@hotmail.com
www.atleticos.tk

Ego Art Centre Madrid, Spain
Author: Agustin Pérez Rubio
Location: The Route of Sense, Gran Via 54, 28013 Madrid, Spain
Date: 12/05/2001

Title: I, in the Botanical Garden Oaxaca
Ego Art Centre in Oaxaca, Mexico
Author: Carmen Cantón
Location: MACO-Museum of Oaxaca's Contemporary Art, Macedonia Alcalá 202, Centro, Oaxaca, 68000, Mexico
Date: 2/9/2003
Carmen Cantón-Ego Art Centre, 2003 - ...
www.crearbosques.org

Title: Manuel Sánchez-Vergara
Ego Art Centre in Cordoba, Argentina
Authors: Soledad Sánchez y Carolina Vergara
Curated by: Luz Novillo Corvalán
Location: Spanish Cultural Centre in Cordoba, Entre Rios 40 - (5000) Cordoba, Argentina
Date: From June 26 until July 17, 2003
Soledad Sánchez-Ego Art Centre, 2003 - ...
ojoporojo@hotmail.com
info@ccec.org.ar

Title: f(l)oros.
Ego Art Centre in Lima, Peru
Author: José-Carlos Mariátegui
Curated by: Jorge Villacorta
Location: Cultural Centre of the Spanish Embassy in Lima,
Natalio Sánchez 181-185, Santa Beatriz, Lima, Peru
José Carlos Mariátegui Museum. Jr. Washington 1938-1946, Lima I (Cercado)
Date: 23/4/2003 - 17.00h
centrocultural@aeci.org.pe
jcm@rcp.net.pe
http://www.rcp.net.pe/MARIATEGUI

Title: Ego Art Centre in Venice
About Contemporary Spanish Art - Ophelia and Ulysses. Venice Biennale, Italy
Author: Carmen Cantón
Location: Pavilionof the Antichi Granei of the Giudecca. Venice, Italy.
Date: juny de 2001
Carmen Cantón-Ego Art Centre 2001 - ...
www.larutadelsentido.org

Title: Food Altar
Ego Art Centre in Lima, Peru
Authors: Juan Peralta Berrios y Jorge Villacorta
Curated by: Jorge Villacorta
Location: Cultural Centre of the Spanish Embassy in Lima,
Natalio Sánchez Lima, Peru
Date: 12/4/2003 - 20:00h
Jorje Villacorta-Ego Art Centre, 2003 - ...
centrocultural@aeci.org.pe
lupe41@hotmail.com
villacorta@yahoo.es

Title: Wedding Fati and Juan Pablo
Ego Art Centre in Rosario, Argentina
Author: Topacio Fresh
Location: The Route of Sense, Gran Via 54, 28013 Madrid, Spain
Date: 27/02/2005
Juan Pablo Arbalsche-Ego Art Centre, 2003 - ...
topacio50@hotmail.com
www.youtube.com

Title: Naturaleza Muerta
Ego Art Centre in Lima, Peru
Author: Maria Fe Nevares
Curated by: Jorge Villacorta
Location: Cultural Centre of the Spanish Embassy in Lima,
Natalio Sánchez 181-185, Santa Beatriz, Lima, Peru
Date: 22/4/2003
centrocultural@aeci.org.pe
mariflex@hotmail.com
www.caretas.com.pe

Title: I, Museum
I. Museum-Ego Art Centre in the MARCO of Vigo, Spain
Curated by: Carmen Cantón
Location: MARCO - Museum of Contemporary Art of Vigo, Príncipe 54, 36202 Vigo, Pontevedra, Spain
Date: 17/12/2004 - 27/02/2005
Ego Art Centre-Irene González Blanco, Amaya González Reyes, Cristina Iglesias Reyes, Diana Lores Nieto y Jorge Migoya, 2006 - ...
www.marcovigo.com

Title: Collection of Museums
Ego Art Centre in Lima, Peru
Author: Emilio Tarazona
Curated by: Jorge Villacorta
Location: Cultural Center of the Spanish Embassy in Lima,
Natalio Sánchez 181-185, Santa Beatriz, Lima, Peru
Date: 22/4/2003
centrocultural@aeci.org.pe
etarazona@post.com

Title: Naturaleza Muerta
Ego Art Centre in Lima, Peru
Author: Maria Fe Nevares
Curated by: Jorge Villacorta
Location: Cultural Centre of the Spanish Embassy in Lima,
Natalio Sánchez 181-185, Santa Beatriz, Lima, Peru
Date: 22/4/2003
centrocultural@aeci.org.pe
mariflex@hotmail.com
www.caretas.com.pe

Title: Further Reductions
Ego Art Centre in Lima, Peru
Author: Carlos León-Xjimenez
Curated by: Jorge Villacorta
Location: Informal shopping center (in industrial ex-place) in Tacora's context (street market of objects in disuse and of the second hand).
Cultural Centre of the Spanish Embassy in Lima,
Natalio Sánchez 181-185, Santa Beatriz, Lima, Peru
Date: 23/4/2003 - 09:00h - 14:45h
cleonxjimenez@gmail.com
www.geocities.com/carlosleons

Romeo & Juliet
Fashion   Design

David Barath
Design and Visual
Group Budapest
Budapest, Hungary

Title
Romeo & Juliet Fashion and Design Store

Client
Romeo & Juliet Fashion and Design Store

Art Director
David Barath

Designer
David Barath

Year Produced
2007

Description
A complete identity design for a fashion and design store.

The client asked for a logo that is modern and fashionable, emotional and international, yet is able to recall the elements of traditional Hungarian folk art while it has to be decorative enough to represent the store without any other additional elements.

Santos&Karlovich™

Amsterdam, The Netherlands

Title
Selected Works of Pauline St. Denis

Client
Pauline St. Denis

Designer
Santos&Karlovich™

Year Produced
2007

Description
The design concept for Pauline St. Denis was to create a limited edition series of books in a really beautiful package. Metallic gold overlay and embossing are used on the box and also the cover of the book.

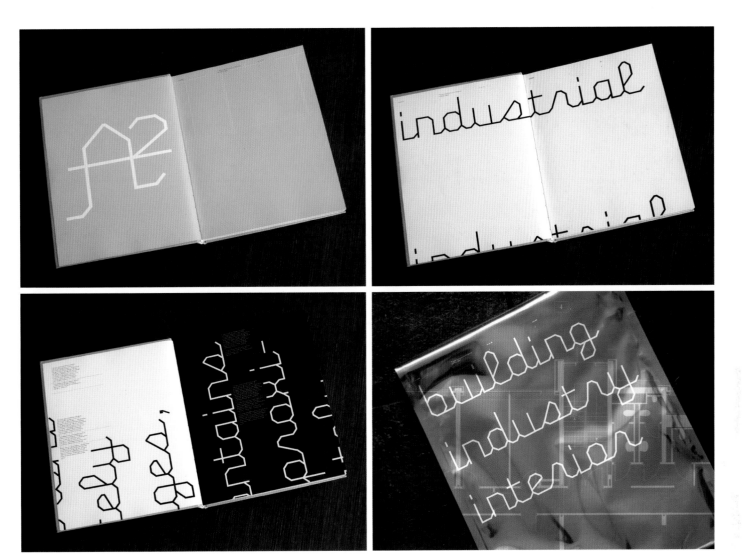

3group
Poznan, Poland

Title
CDF Architekci

Client
CDF Architekci

Art Director
Ryszard Bienert

Designer
Ryszard Bienert

Year Produced
2007

Description
Metallic foil catalogue with silk screen
printed envelope.

Purpose Ltd
London, UK

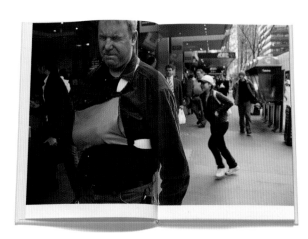

Title
Wounded

Client
Jesse Marlow

Art Director
Rob Howsam

Designer
Rob Howsam, Charlotte Cline

Year Produced
2005

Description
The obsessive Melbourne-based photographer Jesse Marlow takes pictures of people with injuries – the walking wounded, spotting bandages, plasters, crutches and casts. He asked Purpose to help him turning this strange collection of images into a beautiful book. The design is a flesh-tone-padded book protected by a plaster cast style slip case signed by Marlow. Inside, the book borrows further from the medical world using icons and fine paper similar to that found in medicine packaging.

*

**

DRAFT Co., Ltd
Tokyo, Japan

Title
* One Plus One ** Clossing

Client
proponere

Art Director
Yoshie Watanabe

Designer
Yoshie Watanabe

Illustrator
Yoshie Watanabe

Year Produced
2005

Description
This is a book-style package for a wedding and engagement ring.

A marriage certificate and the lyric for the ring's owner are placed on the first few pages while the ring is placed tightly on a base made of felt on the 'last page.'

Stiletto nyc
New York, USA & Milano, Italy

Title	Description
Graphic identity for a high-end children's clothing boutique	Store logo and graphic identity for a new high-end children's clothing store in Bassano, Italy.
Client	
Cenerino	Store design by Andrea Tognon Architecture, Stiletto nyc designed a vintage inspired logo mark to offset the modern store design.
Art Director	
Stiletto nyc	
Designer	
Stiletto nyc	
Year Produced	
2007	

Bibliothèque
London, UK

Title
Catriona Mackechnie identity and packaging

Client
Catriona Mackechnie

Art Director
Tim Beard, Jonathon Jeffrey, Mason Wells

Designer
Tim Beard, Jonathon Jeffrey, Mason Wells

Year Produced
2005

Description
Stationery and packaging for a lingerie store in New York's fashionable meat packing district. The client wanted a timeless, elegant and feminine identity.

A redrawn version of Bodoni Poster combined with a custom-made ligature between the 'c' and 'k' of MacKechnie created a unique feminine marque. To add visual interest, each element was given its own photographic composition of flora, transparent, delicate and precious. This acted as a metaphor for lingerie, and gave a rich and varied visual palette.

Bluemark Inc
Tokyo, Japan

Title
National Standard Shopping Bags

Client
National Standard Inc.

Designer
Atsuki Kikuchi

Illustrator
Atsuki Kikuchi

Year Produced
2005

Description
Series of shopping bags for the Japanese
fashion brand National Standard.

Bluemark Inc
Tokyo/Japan

Title
National Standard Shopping Bags

Client
National Standard Inc.

Designer
Atsuki Kikuchi

Illustrator
Atsuki Kikuchi

Year Produced
2004-2005

Description
Series of shopping bags for the Japanese
fashion brand National Standard.

Thorbjørn Ankerstjerne
London, UK

Title
Pharmacy Bags

Client
Apotek

Art Director
Thorbjørn Ankerstjerne

Designer
Thorbjørn Ankerstjerne

Year Produced
2006

Description
The Danish Pharmacy chain Apotek has recently had its identity redesigned and therefore requested a new design for their paper bags.

Ankerstjerne illustrated different types of medical herbs as well as implanting the new typeface and style designed for Apotek. The idea was to dress the paper bags with a nice and fresh feeling, so Apotek's customers would be happy to carry them outside the shops.

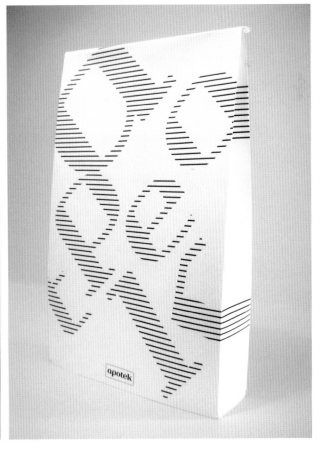

ico design
consultancy ltd.
London, UK

Title
Wedding Stationery

Client
John Lewis

Creative Director
Ben Tomlinson

Art Director
Steve Lloyd

Designer
Andy Spencer

Illustrator
Akira Chatani

Year Produced
2006

Description
ico design's self-promotion piece for Christmas in a form of wrapping paper caught the
eye of John Lewis. Impressed by the inven-
tiveness of the idea, the client approached
ico design for creative treatments for a new
range of wedding products.

The chosen 'love birds' design was sourced
from an original Japanese illustration and
was applied across stationery and a full range
of gift packaging in an appropriate colour
scheme of ivory and gold.

wedding invitation

...ance

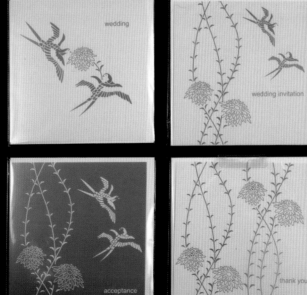

wedding

wedding invitation

acceptance

thank you

SEA
London, UK

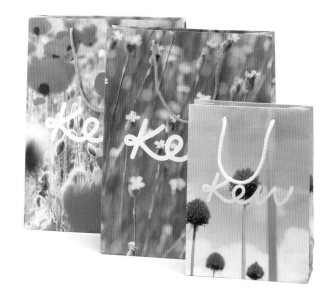

Title
Kew Identity and packaging

Client
Kew / Jigsaw

Art Director
SEA

Designer
SEA

Year Produced
2004

Description
Execution of identity across print, packaging, online and in-store for a high street consumer brand Jigsaw.

 Acne Art Dept
Stockholm, Sweden

Title
Acne Jeans Packaging

Client
Acne Jeans

Art Director
Daniel Carlsten, Jonas Jansson

Designer
Daniel Carlsten, Jonas Jansson

Year Produced
2006

Description
Creative studios, creative process and the actual products are all sources of inspiration to the packaging and communication of Acne Jeans. Some packaging items even share the same buttons, laces or textiles with the clothes they are supposed to carry.

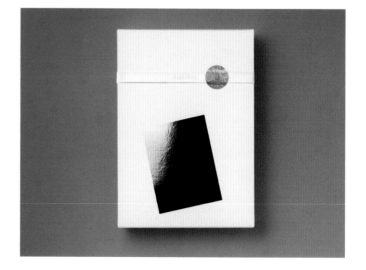

Julia Hoffmann
New York, USA

Title	**Description**
TBSP (Tablespoon)	This was a student project at the School of Visual Arts in New York. The assignment was to create an identity for a store.
Client	
Julia Hoffmann (Self-initiated project)	TBSP is a store that sells spices as well as things around the kitchen. TBSP, the acronym for Tablespoon, is a measurement tool that is unique to cooking.
Art Director	
Julia Hoffmann	
Designer	
Julia Hoffmann	
Year Produced	
2002	

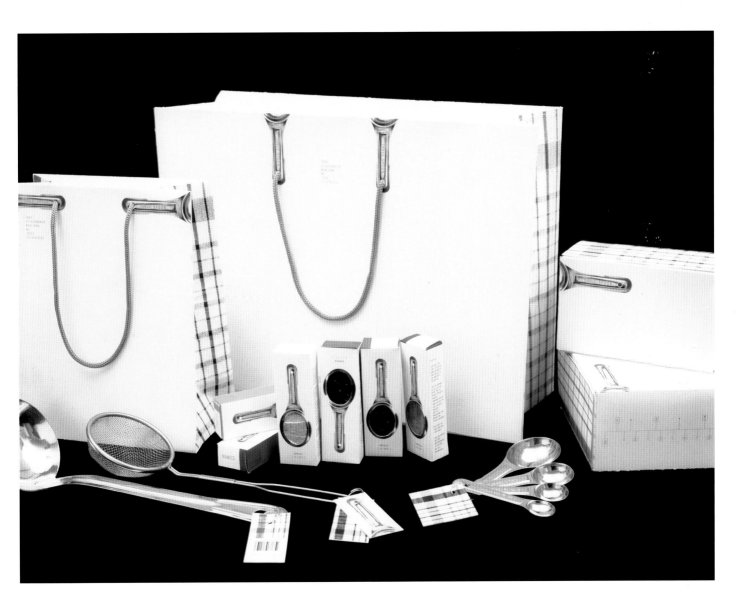

Bas Brand
Identity
Stockholm, Sweden

Title
Living and Giving concept

Client
Inspiration

Art Director
Stefan Sundström, Linnea Lofjord

Creative Director
Marie Wollbeck

Designer
Stefan Sundström

Year Produced
2005

Description
The 'Living and Giving' concept is about combining an offer of products which are exclusive and of high quality, with more accessible, quick turnaround and seasonal products.

The aim for this brand was to be at the top of people's minds for gift buying and to inspire customers to always find something great to give away or bring home, whether small or large.

Bas created a pattern built of products from the Inspiration range. The pattern was used as an identification of Inspiration both in packaging and in-store.

The task was to create a giftable packaging-solution that should not take longer than seconds to wrap. The logo was created with a combination of visability and inspiration that grows.

Thorbjørn Ankerstjerne
London, UK

Title
Bio Bag

Client
College brief

Art Director
Thorbjørn Ankerstjerne

Designer
Thorbjørn Ankerstjerne

Year Produced
2006

Description
6 billion plastic bags are being used every year in the UK. Ankerstjerne finds it extremely appealling that every time when people go to a supermarket in the UK, one would walk out with 3 plastic bags, which is in poor quality. That means, people would throw them right away after having carried the groceries home.

This bag is meant to raise this argument with its bold typographical message being the bag itself.

DFraile

Madrid, Spain

Title
FURNITURE CONGRESS - DESIGN
AND INNOVATION

Client
Arema & DDI

Art Director
Eduardo del Fraile

Designer
Eduardo del Fraile, David Racci

Year Produced
2006

Description
Development of an image for the third
edition of the congress. Imposed by the
client, the only condition was not to use a
chair as a symbol. But why not play with the
joint shape of a chair and a table and look at
furniture from different points of view?

3er Congreso
de diseño
e innovación
del mueble
y la madera

Programa

9.00 - 9.45h.
Entrega de documentación.

9.45 - 10.30h.
Inauguración.
Francisco Marqués.
Consejero de Industria y Medio Ambiente.

Introducción

10.30 - 11.00h.
Perspectivas internacionales: principales retos de futuro.
Juan Ángel Lafuente.
Profesor Titular Dpto. Finanzas y Contabilidad de la Universitat Jaume I.

11.00 - 11.15h.
Coloquio.

Diseño e Innovación

11.15 - 11.45h.
El diseño: una herramienta de innovación empresarial.
Santiago Miranda. Diseñador, King & Miranda (Milán) Premio Nacional Diseño 1989.

11.45 - 12.15h.
Café.

12.15 - 12.45h.
Las claves para la incorporación del diseño de producto a la empresa.
Ramón Benedito. Diseñador, Premio Nacional Diseño 1992.

12.45 - 13.1...
Diseño adaptado... necesidades del c...
Pedro Vera. Director IBV – de Biomecánica de Valencia

13.15 - 13.45h.
Innovación en madera.
Pilar Calvo Consejera Radisa, (Maderas Raimundo Diaz, SA).

13.45 - 14.00h.
Coloquio.

14.00 - 16.00h.
Almuerzo.

Factores de Éxito

16.00 - 16.30h.
La marca como factor de confianza y fidelización del cliente.
Fernando Ocaña Presidente de FCB/Tapsa.

16.30 - 17.00h.
La internacionalizació... empresa familiar.
Ramón Sanfeli...
Exdesign M...

Para analizar todos los cambios a los que hoy nos enfrentamos para amueblar y decorar los espacios tanto privados como públicos, vamos a profundizar en diferentes aspectos:

Un análisis de la evolución reciente de las principales económicas... y la situación actual de la economía española permitirá determinar las etapas de desarrollo competitivo. Se analizará la coyuntura actual del sector del mueble y los retos de futuro.

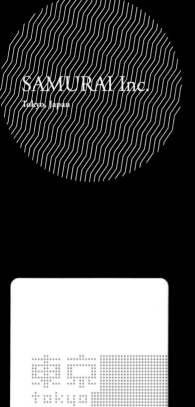

SAMURAI Inc.
Tokyo, Japan

Title
TOKYO BAR

Client / Producer
TRANSIT GENERAL OFFICE INC.

Art Director
Kashiwa Sato

Designer
Gen Eto

Architect
SOLID AIR

Illustrator
MACHCOMIX

Year Produced
2007

Description
The café and bar gathered several elements of Tokyo Pop Culture.

The symbol represents the pop feeling and the sense of speed of Tokyo.

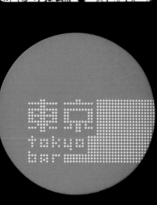

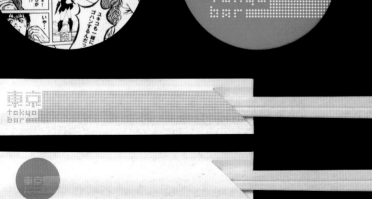

OMD
Contemporary
Design Terminal
Beijing, China

Title
07 Jian

Client
School of Design, Central Academy of Fine Arts

Art Director
Jiang hua

Designer
Jiang hua and students from 11studio of the School of Design, Central Academy of Fine Arts

Year Produced
2007

Description
'07 Jian' was a seven-day graduation exhibition held by the School of Design, Central Academy of Fine Arts in the new building (No.7) of the university. The exhibition had a core exhibition within a seven-floor space and an external outreach of over 10 opening studios.

The designers integrated a visual system for '07 Jian,' including a range of flexible inter-related elements. Texts in space were the most crucial elements. Based on the characteristics of this exhibition: complexity, short-term, academic and celebration, an easy-operated, character design-cored image system is set up. For flexible usage, they designed different image materials, which can be used individually or jointly, that intervened and converted the original teaching space and could display spatial information.

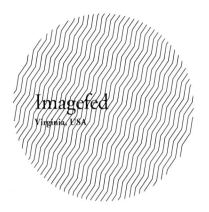

Imagefed
Virginia, USA

Title
Untitled

Client
Bong Vodka

Art Director
Matthew Curry

Designer
Matthew Curry

Year Produced
2006

Description
Josh Spear asked Curry to design a limited edition packaging and labels for the new premiere vodka 'Bong Vodka' along with a selected group of other artists and designers.

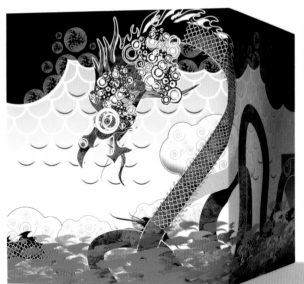

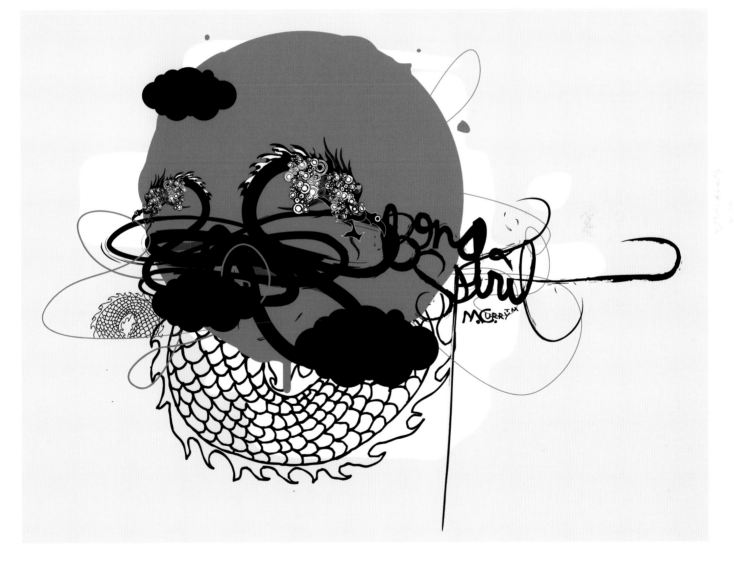

Bluemark Inc
Tokyo, Japan

Title
BP Box

Client
Bluemark

Art Director
Atsuki Kikuchi

Designer
Atsuki Kikuchi

Year Produced
2006

Description
Shipping box for the Bluemark product label
run by Bluemark via bluemark.co.jp.

3group
Poznan, Poland

Title
Pro Arte

Client
Fundacja Pro Arte

Agency
3group

Designer
Ryszard Bienert

Year Produced
2008

Description
When designing the shopping bags for Pro Arte Foundation, Bienert's main aim was to arouse interest and create a characteristic colour code. Bienert emphasised a wide range of promotion activities including art promotion, publishing catalogues etc. to presenting the name of the Foundation in different colours and typefaces from serif to calligraphy and sans serif. Each bag has different design but at the same time refers to the rest.

Bienert applied screen print on the paper bags which achieved a unique effect for each print. An imperfection was therefore used as a trump. This presenatation aroused receivers' interest, the game between repeatibility and difference has provoked receivers to familiarize with certain visual code.

Title
Akiko Yano - 'Hajimete no Yano Akiko' CD
Jacket

Client
Yamaho Communications

Art Director
Atsuki Kikuchi

Designer
Atsuki Kikuchi

Year Produced
2006

Description
Akiko Yano is a major recording artist in Japan. The album 'Hajimete no Yano Akiko' is an anniversary album which features friends of Akiko Yano as guest artists. The concept of different musicians coming together on one album was picked up in the sleeve design where different shapes on different layers form new shapes, shadows and spaces.

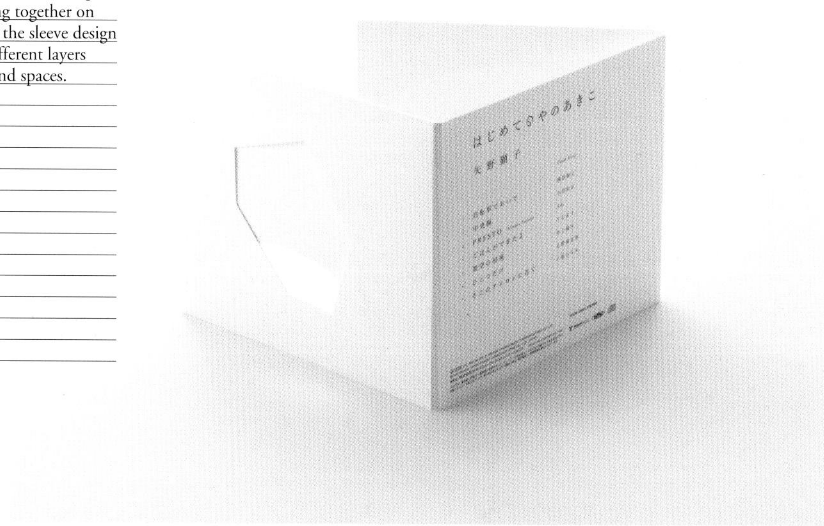

Bluemark Inc.
Tokyo, Japan

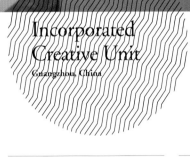

Incorporated
Creative Unit
Guangzhou, China

Title
C Record

Client
Vowelmusic

Art Director
Bai Ganggang

Designer
Bai Ganggang

Year Produced
2006

Description
The first album released by Vowelmusic, it is a collection of works from 20 bands/artists from mainland China, Hong Kong and Taiwan. The material used for the CD jacket is pressed paper pulp of recycled newspaper and cardboard, which is easy to decompose and very environmental friendly. In fact, this material has been widely used for packaging of fragile objects, e.g. eggs and delicate instruments. This could be perceived as an implication that, in the contemporary world, independent music is filled with life, energy and wisdom, yet appears so fragile in front of the hard rules of commercialism. Bai truly wishes that with his own efforts and this eco-friendly design, he will be able to provide music with some form of support, even if it's just as small as a CD jacket.

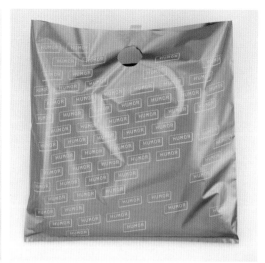

Bluemark Inc
Tokyo, Japan

Title
HUMOR

Client
HUIT Inc.

Designer
Atsuki Kikuchi

Illustrator
Atsuki Kikuchi

Year Produced
2007-08

Description
Branding and packaging items for the Japanese online fashion store, HUMOR.

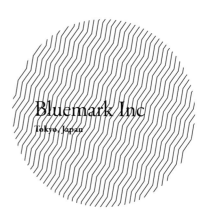

Title
Sally Scott Shopping Bags

Client
LADIES NEWYORKER CO., LTD.

Designer
Atsuki Kikuchi

Illustrator
Atsuki Kikuchi

Year Produced
2007

Description
Shopping bags and shop cards for the Japanese fashion brand, Sally Scott.

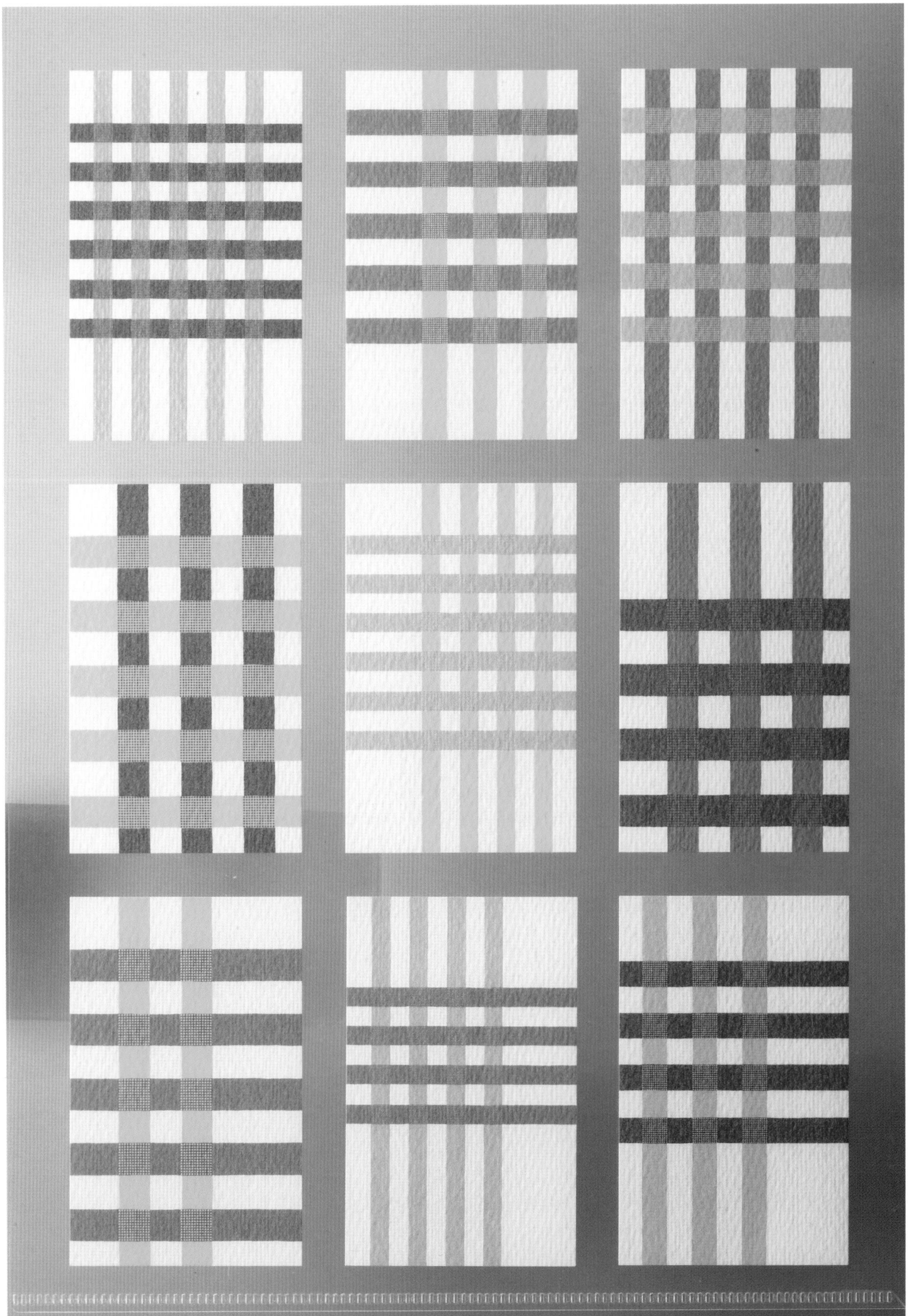

Son of Tam
New York, USA

Title
Studio Collateral - For Office Use Only

Client
For Office Use Only

Creative Director
Anh Tuan Pham

Designer
Jason Tam at Son of Tam

Year Produced
2006

Description
For Office Use Only (FOUO) is a New York-based design studio. In addition to client projects, FOUO develops self-initiated projects just like this photographic series of print collateral, in order to communicate their design aesthetics and sensibilities. These projects represent moments in the on-going visual narrative of FOUO.

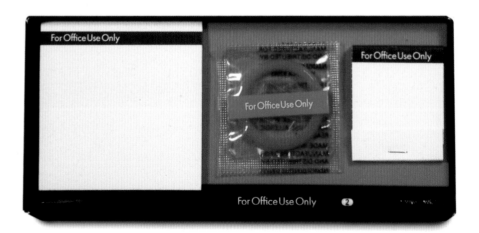

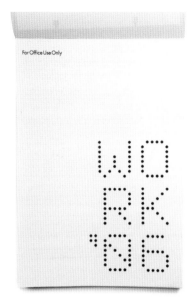

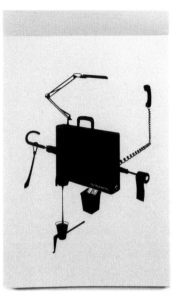

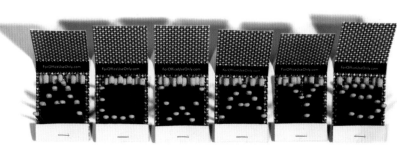

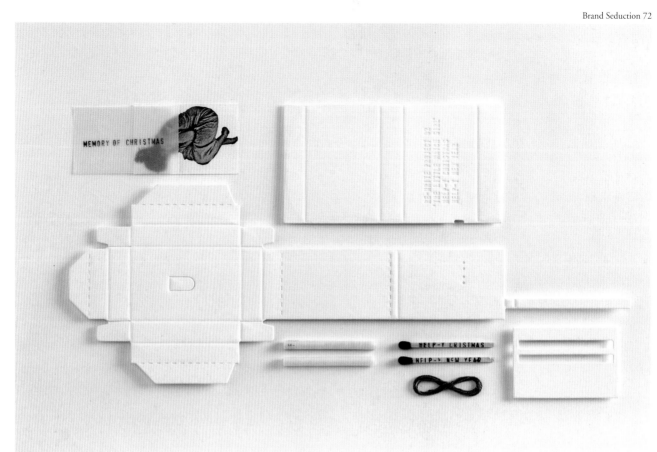

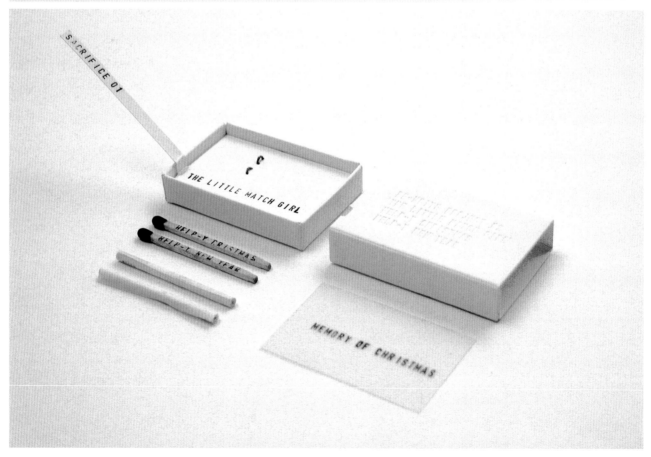

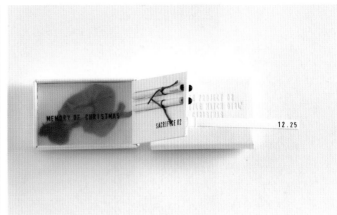

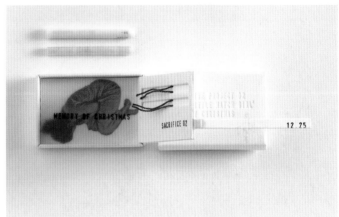

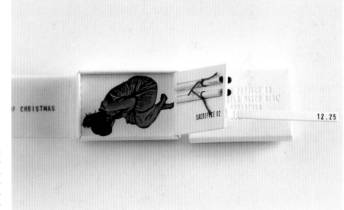

NONAME
NOSHOP
Seoul, Korea

Title
The Little Match Girl (Help-y Christmas &
Help-y new year)

Client
'earth project,' Korea

Art Director
NONAME NOSHOP

Designer
NONAME NOSHOP

Year Produced
2005

Description
Produced as a Christmas gift for the families
and friends of NONAME NOSHOP
designers in 2005, it marks the second in
the series of their 're-write project.' The box
delivered a message that, on Christmas day
we can celebrate the birth of Jesus Christ and
at the same time remember the deaths of the
little match girls. There are two pieces of paper inside the box: a statistical list of Korean
youth families and an empty piece of paper
for rewriting the little match girl's story.

Checkland
Kindleysides
Leicestershire, UK

Title
Levi's Packaging

Client
Levi Strauss

Art Director
Carl Murch, Checkland Kindleysides

Designer
Checkland Kindleysides

Year Produced
2006

Description
Reflecting the Levi's® store interior that is texturally rich, with a premium palette of materials, the designers created in-store packaging with a handcrafted feel.

Carrier bags and gift wrapping were developed using raw materials, an embossed logo, handwritten fonts and simple black & white photography.

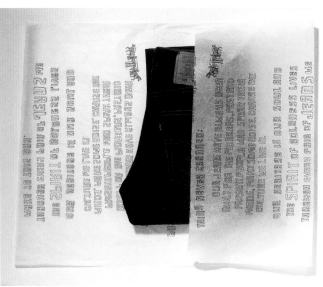

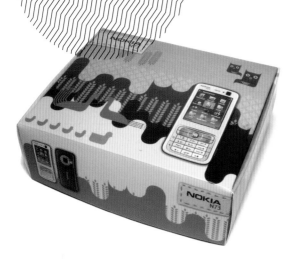

Daniella
Domingues
São Paulo, Brazil

Title
Kinderboerderij

Client
Nokia

Art Director
Daniella Domingues

Designer
Daniella Domingues

Year Produced
2007

Description
For this work, Domingues mixed vectorial illustration with a little hand sewn 'label' and digital fusion.

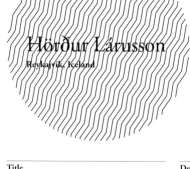

Hörður Lárusson
Reykjavík, Iceland

Title
Bullseye

Client
Hörður Lárusson (Self initiated project)

Art Director
Hörður Lárusson

Designer
Hörður Lárusson

Year Produced
2007

Description
A one-year calander, covering roughly the training year of 2007-08 in 10m Air Pistol shooting. Each week is printed on an actual target used in a recent Air Pistol competition and each target has two shots in it. All the targets are approved by the ISSF.

29 Agency
Texas, USA

Title
TEEL Promotion

Client
TEEL

Art Director
Tyler Merrick, Darren Dunham,
Jonathan Rollins

Designer
Brandon Bargas

Photographer
Ben Rollins

Year Produced
2007

Description
The artist needed a piece that he could send
out to record companies, talent agencies and
the likes that would get their attention. In
today's music market, record labels get tons
of CD's handed to them all of the time. It is
important for the artists to make themselves
stand out and get a second look.

29 AGENCY created a box that looked like
an amp with an actual handle on it that the
artist could fill with promotional material. It
includes pictures, CDs and other information that would be presented as a gift and a
leave behind at the same time.

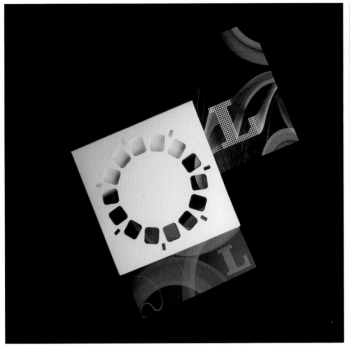

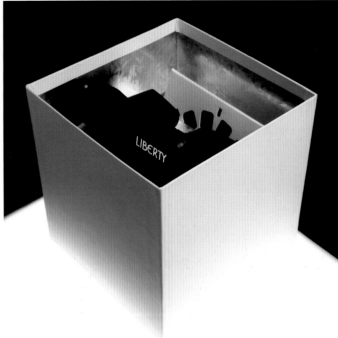

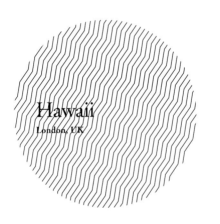

Hawaii
London, UK

Title
Liberty Christmas Press Box

Client
Liberty

Art Director
Tracey De La Marquand, Katie Hind

Designer
Paul McAnelly

Year Produced
2006

Description
Liberty wanted to create a limited edition boxset specifically aimed at the Press. A photo shoot was commissioned to shoot key pieces featured in the Liberty Christmas Shop.

These were then transferred onto two disks that could only be viewed using a vintage viewfinder Hawaii sourced from the U.S.A. Liberty which has a wonderful archive of design and print. The 'L' foiled in silver that Hawaii chose for the front of the box is actually dated back to the 1950's.

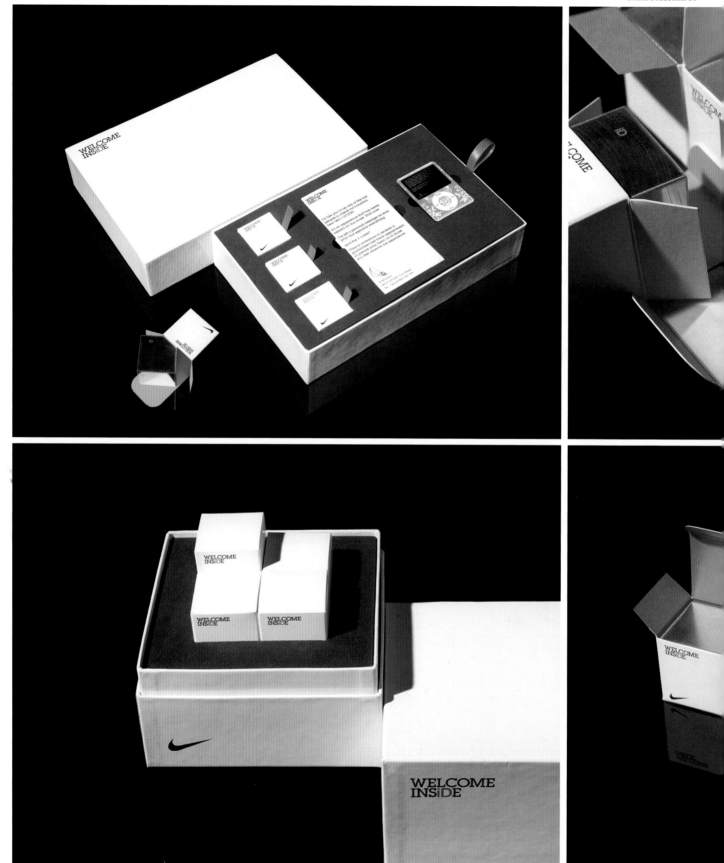

ODD
London, UK

Title
NIKEiD Studio London Invitation

Client
Nike UK

Art Director
Simon Glover, Nick Stickland

Designer
Richard Stevens, Stuart Bailey

Year Produced
2007

Description
ODD were commissioned to design and produce a set of direct mail invitations to launch the NIKEiD London store. The brief was to put Nike iD high on the London agenda and make it an aspirational destination to experience.

The box was sent to 50 of London's key celebrities, each one containing several pieces of inspirational communication: An iPod Nano, each containing a personalised video message from the store concierge. Then, an invitation to the launch party. Finally a set of 3 aluminium 'cube keys,' each one crash numbered with 1 of 1000 unique codes. These cube-keys could be given to a friend, who would then also be granted an exclusive priority consultation at the store.

abraka design
(Traffic)
Lille, France

Title
'la boqueria' Wine Boxes

Client
la boqueria

Art Director
Carine Abraham

Designer
Carine Abraham

Year Produced
2007

Description
Wine packaging for a Spanish restaurant.

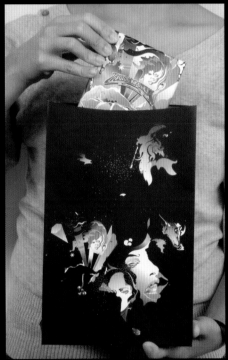

Shya-la-la
Production Ltd.
Hong Kong, China

Title
Rock Candy

Client
Rock Candy

Art Director
Wing Shya, Marcus Savage

Designer
Sarah Yung

Year Produced
2005

Description
The Rock Candy brand is unique and creative in terms of concept, design and target. A Rock is a girls' best friend and it is so sweet that it tastes like candy. The rock's glamourous lifestyle is associated with free spirited individualism, and the youthful adventure in each one of us, much like its choice of bold and free colours. So the stylish and colourful illustration of women with different emotions and facets, surrounded by 'tiny' diamonds, easily communicate this kind of lifestyle.

Rock Candy is originally based in Asia, yet, due to its unique and adventurous interplay of colours and graphics in its jewelry design, packaging and concept, the development of the brand is already stepping through the international threshold.

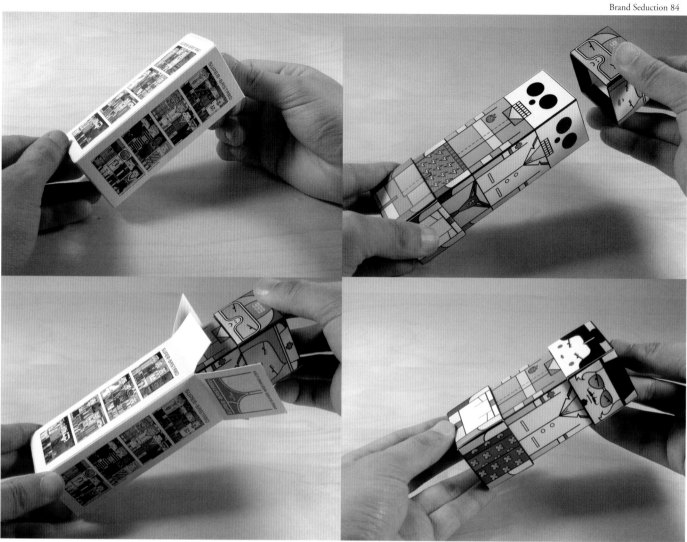

Undoboy
Oregon Portland

Title
Super Bastard Box Art Character

Client
Undoboy

Art Director
Undoboy

Designer
Undoboy

Year Produced
2006

Description
Super-Bastard Box Art Characters consists of 16 unique toys in one set, with 4 unique characters on each face of the box. Collectors have an opportunity to collect all 16 toys / 64 characters in the series. They are colourful and fun to play with. Each toy has 4 characters with a custom-designed suit so that collectors can interchange their heads and pants with different bodies.

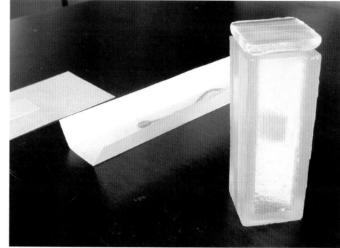

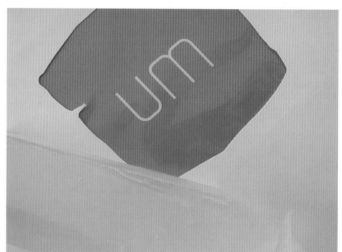

Bread and Butter SA
Lausanne, Switzerland

Title
UM Collection

Client
H.Stern Jewellery

Creative Director / Art Director
Cristiana Bolli Freitas

Product Designer
Laurent Bolli

Graphic Designer
Cédric Henny

Ceramist
Valérie Alonso

Year Produced
2002

Description
It's a jewel collection packaging in 4 different formats made out of a special bluish glass. The packaging is composed by a silkscreened thin paper wrapping up the jewel, a glass box, a transparent rubber string and a small bag with specific tissue with the logo.

The packaging was designed for a new, young jewel collection named 'UM,' which means 'one' in Brazilian Portuguese. The kind of jewel in UM collection is gold and white gold with small diamonds.

The production process was quite innovative because it applied a ceramic technique onto glass. It was developed in Switzerland and the technology was transferred to Brazil for large production.

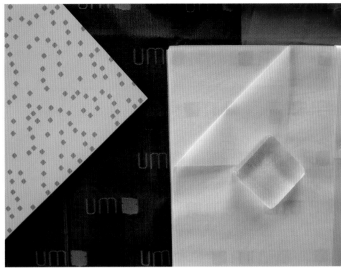

lifestyle stimuli
lifestyle stimulans
estímulos de la forma de vida
生活的刺激
ライフスタイル×刺激
생활양식의 자극

Our container culture extends to packing things that may do well or look good on their own. Wallpaper-patterned toiletry bottles and comic illustrations on t-shirt, sneakers, stationery and CD packs are some of the attempts to enhance the status of the seemingly mundane everyday products. This section is a glimpse of how packaging is going increasingly eco- and user-conscious.

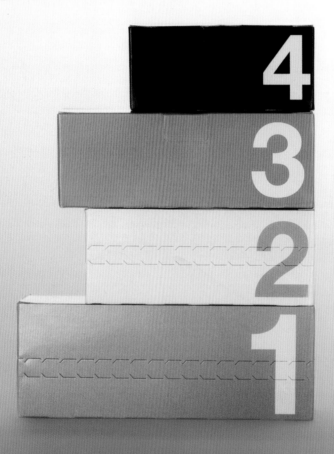

Stockholm
Design Lab
Stockholm, Sweden

Title
Askul Design and Packaging Concept

Client
Askul

Designer
Stockholm Design Lab

Year Produced
2005 Ongoing

Description
Stockholm Design Lab has created a comprehensive design program for Askul that covers corporate identity, product development and design, and packaging solutions. The main objective of the new identity is to increase Askul's competitive power and brand heat in a mature market. The ambition is to mark the introduction of a new era and communicate the evolution of the Askul company.

Askul
Office Cleaner
オフィスのおそうじ
しつこい汚れ落としシート
Microfiber Wet Tissue
For tough stains

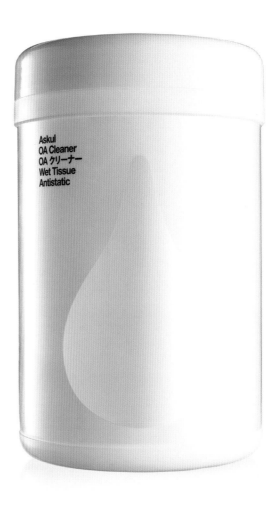

Askul
OA Cleaner
OA クリーナー
Wet Tissue
Antistatic

Stockholm
Design Lab
Stockholm, Sweden

Title
Askul Design and Packaging Concept

Client
Askul

Designer
Stockholm Design Lab

Year Produced
2005 Ongoing

Description
Stockholm Design Lab has created a comprehensive design program for Askul that covers corporate identity, product development and design, and packaging solutions. The main objective of the new identity is to increase Askul's competitive power and brand heat in a mature market. The ambition is to mark the introduction of a new era and communicate the evolution of the Askul company.

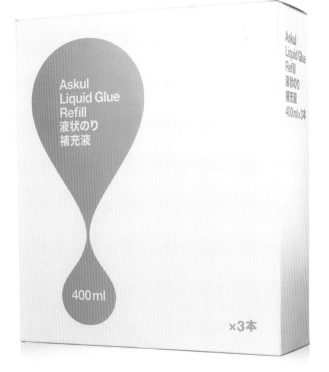

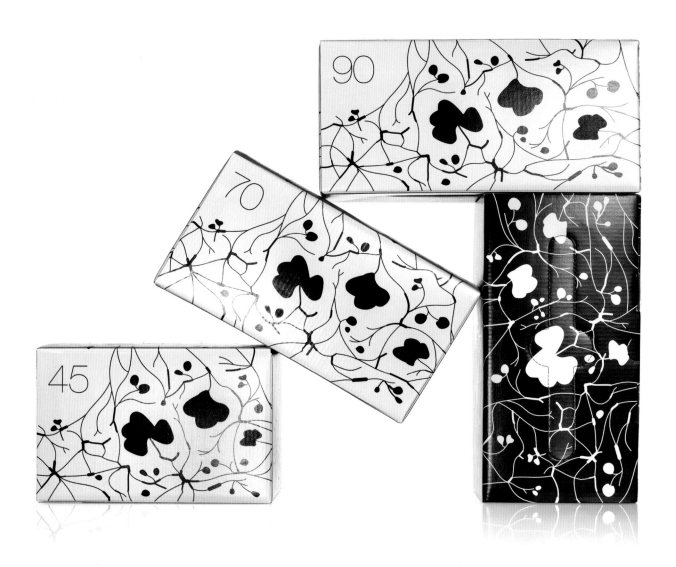

Stockholm
Design Lab
Stockholm, Sweden

Title
Askul Design and Packaging Concept

Client
Askul

Designer
Stockholm Design Lab

Year Produced
2005 Ongoing

Description
Stockholm Design Lab has created a comprehensive design program for Askul that covers corporate identity, product development and design, and packaging solutions. The main objective of the new identity is to increase Askul's competitive power and brand heat in a mature market. The ambition is to mark the introduction of a new era and communicate the evolution of the Askul company.

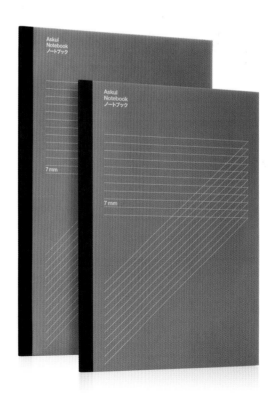

Askul
Ink Jet Paper
インクジェットペーパー
写真用光沢紙
Photo
Cast Coated Gloss
A3

Askul
Ink Jet Paper
インクジェットペーパー
写真用マット紙 両面
Photo Matt Coated
A3

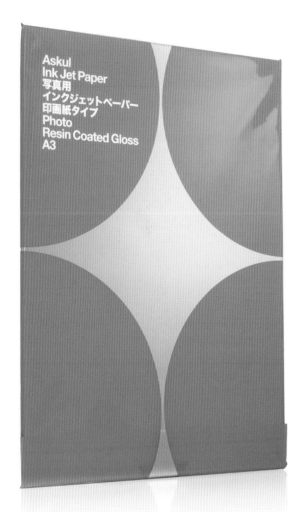

Askul
Ink Jet Paper
写真用
インクジェットペーパー
印画紙タイプ
Photo
Resin Coated Gloss
A3

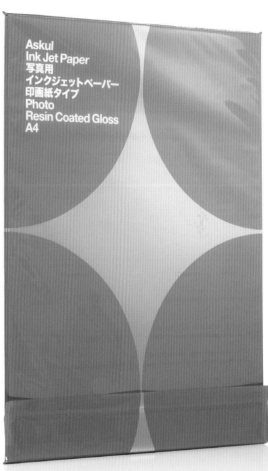

Askul
Ink Jet Paper
写真用
インクジェットペーパー
印画紙タイプ
Photo
Resin Coated Gloss
A4

Stockholm
Design Lab
Stockholm, Sweden

Title
Askul Design and Packaging Concept

Client
Askul

Designer
Stockholm Design Lab

Year Produced
2005 Ongoing

Description
Stockholm Design Lab has created a comprehensive design program for Askul that covers corporate identity, product development and design, and packaging solutions. The main objective of the new identity is to increase Askul's competitive power and brand heat in a mature market. The ambition is to mark the introduction of a new era and communicate the evolution of the Askul company.

Title
Askul Design and Packaging Concept

Client
Askul

Designer
Stockholm Design Lab

Year Produced
2005 Ongoing

Description
Stockholm Design Lab has created a comprehensive design program for Askul that covers corporate identity, product development and design, and packaging solutions. The main objective of the new identity is to increase Askul's competitive power and brand heat in a mature market. The ambition is to mark the introduction of a new era and communicate the evolution of the Askul company.

Stockholm
Design Lab
Stockholm, Sweden

Turner
Duckworth
London, UK & San Francisco, USA

Title
Camera Film

Client
Superdrug Stores Plc.

Agency
Turner Duckworth

Creative Director
David Turner, Bruce Duckworth

Designer
Sarah Moffat

Year Produced
2002

Description
The overlapping circles motif was created for Superdrug's own brand camera films. It shows the mixing of primary light colours, a basic in the science of the photographic process. The motif is positioned on the corner of the boxes and on the backing card. The colours are rotated to differentiate 200 ISO/400 ISO and APS.

Title
Askul

Client
Askul

Art Director
Susanna Nygren Barrett

Designer
Mia Heijkenskjöld, Martin Frostner

Year Produced
2006-07

Description
Askul is one of Japan's fastest growing companies. Its products include everything from furniture to computers, food and office supply.

To further strengthen Askul's own line of products, BVD was appointed to design a number of products for the international cooperation. Using Scandinavian design as a starting point, the product's function, simplicity, and clarity was made to stand out in its redesigned appearance.

BVD's goal was to make the products visible through the packaging allowing them to stand out in the extensive product catalogue as well as looking attractive in home and office.

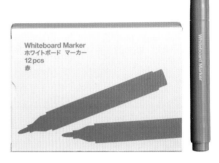

D'Fraile
Madrid, Spain

Title
ContainerBook

Client
Silvia Arce Moreno

Art Director
Eduardo del Fraile

Designer
Eduardo del Fraile, David Racci

Year Produced
2005

Description
A book which presents the norms for recycling, and explains the what, where and why of separating the waste for its later recycling.

With a shape that represents a container which explains its contents, the book is divided into four sections: Paper and cardboard, Light packaging, Glass containers, and Ecopark. Each one of them has its corresponding representative colour.

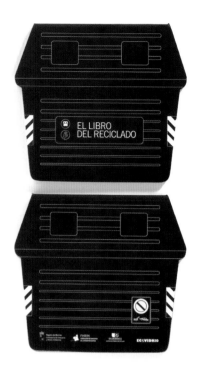

DEPOSITAMOS
EL PAPEL (FOLIOS), PAPEL DE REGALO, FOLLETOS
DE PUBLICIDAD...), LOS PERIÓDICOS, LAS REVISTAS,
EMBALAJES Y LOS ENVASES DE CARTÓN COMO CAJAS
DE GALLETAS, CEREALES...

NO DEPOSITAMOS
GRAPAS, CLIPS, CUBIERTAS DE PLÁSTICO, PORTAFOLIOS,
PAPEL/CARTÓN PLASTIFICADO O ENCERADO, SOBRES CON VENTANAS,
Y LO QUE NO SEA ESTRICTAMENTE PAPEL O CARTÓN.

**PAPEL
Y CARTÓN**

CÓMO
DOBLAR EL PAPEL
O PLEGAR EL CARTÓN,
E INTRODUCIRLO EN EL
CONTENDEDOR, SIN BOLSA.

DEPOSITAMOS
LATAS (REFRESCOS, CERVEZAS, CONSERVAS...),
LOS ENVASES DE BRIK COMO LA LECHE O EL ZUMO;
Y LOS ENVASES DE PLÁSTICO DE ALIMENTACIÓN
(BANDEJAS, BOTELLAS DE AGUA,
DE ZUMOS...), DE LIMPIEZA (DETERGENTES,
SUAVIZANTES...) Y DE HIGIENE (CHAMPÚS, GELES...).

NO DEPOSITAMOS
PAÑALES, RESTOS DE COMIDA, PAPEL Y CARTÓN, JUGUETES,
CINTAS DE VÍDEO, BOMBILLAS.

**ENVASES
LIGEROS**

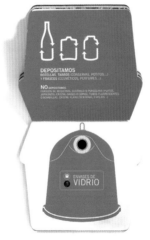

DEPOSITAMOS
BOTELLAS, TARROS (CONSERVAS, POTITOS...),
Y FRASCOS (COSMÉTICOS, PERFUMES...).

NO DEPOSITAMOS
FRASCOS DE MEDICINAS, GUANTES O PORCELANA ROTA,
JARRONES, CRISTAL (VASOS O COPAS), TUBOS FLUORESCENTES
O BOMBILLAS, CRISTAL PLANO (DE VENTANAS, ESPEJOS...).

**ENVASES DE
VIDRIO**

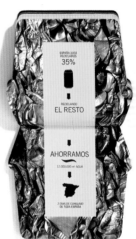

ESPAÑA 2003
RECICLAMOS
35%

RECICLANDO
EL RESTO

AHORRAMOS
12.000.000 m³ AGUA

2 DÍAS DE CONSUMO
DE TODA ESPAÑA

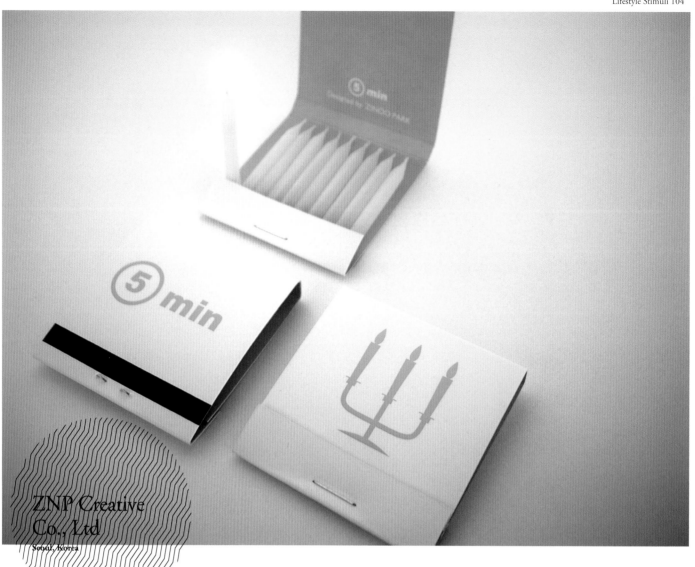

Title
5 Minute Candles

Client
Zinoo Park (Self-initiated project)

Art Director
Zinoo Park

Designer
Zinoo Park

Year Produced
2004

Description
Ten small pocket candles made to celebrate happy moments. Users can keep them in their pockets, so they don't need to worry about forgetting their friends' birthdays or anniversaries. Each candle burns for approximately 5 minutes.

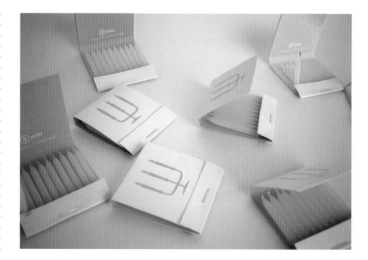

Elisabeth Soós
Graz, Austria

Title
T-Pod

Client
Elisabeth Soós (Self-initiated project)

Art Director
Elisabeth Soós

Designer
Elisabeth Soós, Florian Nissl

Year Created
2006

Description
Firstly take the tea bag out of the box, then unfold it to make it a little boat; put it into the cup with hot water and let it swim around until the tea is ready.

Stockholm Design Lab
Stockholm, Sweden

Title
Rörstrand Design and Packaging Concept

Client
Rörstrand

Designer
Stockholm Design Lab

Year Produced
2002-03

Description
Rörstrand was founded in 1726 and is Sweden's oldest porcelain manufacturer and the second oldest porcelain manufacturer in Europe. Today, the company is a part of the iittala Group.

Stockholm Design Lab helped Rörstrand launch a range of new wine glasses. They designed a transparent packaging that displayed the product directly, without unpacking it. The packaging also helped the retailers create a more efficient instore administration.

Homework
Copenhagen K, Denmark

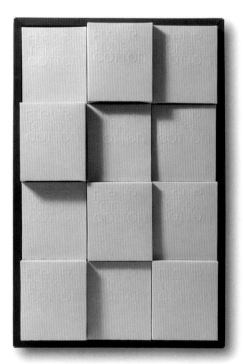

Title
Fleur Tang

Client
Fleur Tang

Product Designer
Fleur Tang

Art Director
Jack Dahl

Graphic Designer
Jack Dahl

Photographer
© Photography Nicky de Silva

Year Produced
2007 Ongoing

Description
Fleur Tang garment and packaging is made of 100% organic materials. From the cotton to the mills to the manufacturing, every process is done with the environment in mind – and without harmful chemicals. A piece of clothing with peace of mind.

Sarah Cihat
New York, USA

Title
* Floral Facet Cups
** Perfume in Porcelain

Client
* Sarah Cihat (Self-initiated project)
** Joya Candle

Art Director
* Sarah Cihat
** Sarah Cihat, Frederick Bouchardy

Designer
* Sarah Cihat
** Sarah Cihat, Frederick Bouchardy

Year Produced
* 2006 ** 2007

Description
* The cups, diffusers, and candleholders are made of hand cast white and black porcelain, based on shapes the designer created. Cihat made molds of each shape to produce multiples. Decals were then created to decorate the cups differently, while the candle decals specify different scents. The cup decals are based on flowers Cihat drew. She then scanned them into Photoshop and shaped them into silhouettes she had previously created. The candle and diffuser decals and package design were researched then generated in Photoshop and Illustrator with her partner and Joya Candle's owner, Frederick Bouchardy.

** A project designed with Cihat's friend, Frederick Bouchardy, for the home fragrance market. Each of the six scents has its own motif to accompanying on both the vessel itself and the packaging, which is adorned with thorns and ribbons. Sarah designed the vessels with soft facets that allow the motifs to appear more than one surface.

Kinetic

Singapore

Title
Kinetic Refill Bottles

Client
Kinetic, Singapore

Creative Director
Pann Lim, Roy Poh

Art Director
Leng Soh, Pann Lim, Roy Poh

Writer
Eugene Tan

Year Produced
2007

Description
Kinetic believes that everyone encounters dirt every day, as well as run-of-the-mill designs for detergents of sorts. Detergents off the shelves come in packaging that are either too gaudy or boring, until now. There is a sizeable number of consumers who appreciate products that have differentiation and are aesthetically pleasing to the eye. After all, what we buy reflects, in many ways, who we are.

We face different cleaning challenges every day. These situations are reflected in the packaging designs where you see the toughest of stains. But what makes it easy on the eye is an aesthetically pleasing refill bottle, which Kinetic specially designed, manufactured and packaged to allow discerning consumers to fill with detergent of their choice.

Jesse Kirsch
New Jersey, USA

Title
Tazaa Soap

Client
Tazaa

Art Director
Jesse Kirsch

Designer
Jesse Kirsch

Year Produced
2006

Description
Strong typography and a sharp colour palette define this packaging system for a line of 6 scented soaps. The bright white of the sleeve evokes a feeling of cleanliness, while the interior box conveys the colour of the ingredients used to make the soap. The initials of each scent's name die cut on the outside sleeve allow the colour of the box below to show through. A small narrow opening at either end invites the consumer to smell the soap without having the box opened. The product itself echoes its packaging with matching initials recessed into the surface of each bar.

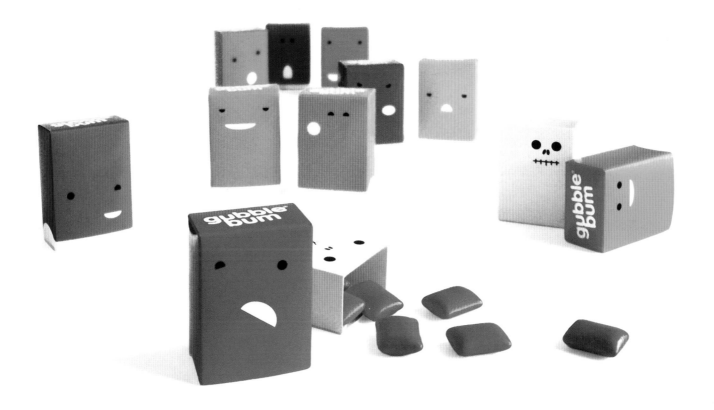

Jesse Kirsch
New Jersey, USA

Title
Gubble Bum Bubble Gum

Client
Gubble Bum

Art Director
Jesse Kirsch

Designer
Jesse Kirsch

Year Produced
2007

Description
A fun and twisted approach to packaging for a line of flavored bubble gum. The characters are comprised of nothing more than full and half circles; yet despite this extreme simplicity, their faces still manage to convey a wide range of emotions. Beneath the cutesy exterior, however, lies an unexpected twist: removing the outer box reveals the skeleton of each 'bum.'

Pearlfisher
London, UK & New York, USA

Title
Cowshed

Client
Cowshed

Art Director
Karen Wellman

Designer
Karen Wellman

Year Produced
2005

Description
Pearlfisher was asked to redesign Soho House's Cowshed range of hair and body products, which would be sold at selected stores on the high street, Pearlfisher's key task was to capture and communicate the Soho House experience on-pack.

The design uses Babington House as its source – reinterpreting its wallpapered interiors into stunning pieces of packaging. Pattern, colour and texture is cleverly used to echo the benefit and ingredient of each product, effortlessly relocating the country house experience from Babington to users' bathroom. Even the mischievous product names and copies are distillations of the Soho House attitude. Its playful sense of humour and easygoing nature is as relaxed as a weekend away – and a far cry from the overblown language of traditional luxury.

Pearlfisher
London, UK & New York, USA

Title
Umi

Client
Waitrose

Art Director
Shaun Bowen

Designer
Natalie Chung

Year Produced
2005

Description
This is a package design for Waitrose's latest range of premium toiletries – umi. As the ingredients for umi are sourced from nature including plants, flowers and food products, Pearlfisher decided to work with a 'gourmet toiletries' theme. The design uses elements of premium food packaging to convey a sense of luxury, provenance and perfection to the range.

Pearlfisher carefully selected the packaging structures that are reminiscent of food packaging. Simple shapes and finishes gives the range a kind of minimal appeal associated with many luxury brands, pink and grey design enhances this. By focusing on the aromas and textures of the product, the copy also echoes food packaging and names such as 'body soufflé' and 'intensive conditioner for hungry hair' emphasise this.

Ryszard Bienert
Poznań, Portland

Title
Moistening Balm

Client
Soraya

Art Director
Ryszard Bienert

Designer
Ryszard Bienert

Year Produced
2005

Description
Design of cosmetics packaging series
- Cleansing tonic – moistening / stimulant.
These are prototypes of transparent plastic
bottles.

Ryszard Bienert
Poznan, Portland

Title
Cleansing Tonic – Moistening / Timulant

Client
Soraya

Art Director
Ryszard Bienert

Designer
Ryszard Bienert

Illustrator
Eboy

Year Produced
2005

Description
Design of cosmetics packaging series
- Cleansing tonic – moistening / stimulant.
These are prototypes of transparent plastic
bottles.

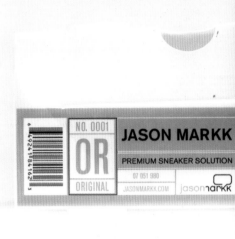

Chhun Tang
California, USA

Title
Jason Markk Premium Sneaker Solution

Client
Jason Markk

Designer
Chhun Tang, April Larivee

Year Produced
2007

Description
The client, Jason Markk came up with some really good ideas from the start so the designers worked with a great foundation. Packaging a sneaker cleaning solution in a scaled-down sneaker box made too much sense. The look and feel revolved around the box and the box label, which carried onto the bottle. Jason also wanted a recognizable image for the box itself and threw out the idea of koi. The designers tried different approaches to the koi and the final were paint splatters, a more suggestive form that was inspired by art and street culture.

Broadhong
Seoul, Korea

Title
Rolling Band-aid

Client
Jaehyung Hong

Art Director
Jaehyung Hong

Designer
Jaehyung Hong

Year Produced
2007

Description
The paper cover of protecting the adhesion of Band-Aids usually creates a lot of wastes. Thus, this band-aids is re-designed in a roll form which is environmental-friendly as it reduces the paper waste. Furthermore, the shipping expenses can be reduced by one-third at maximum.

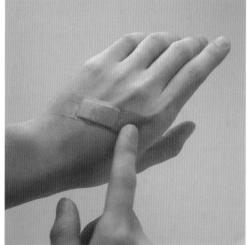

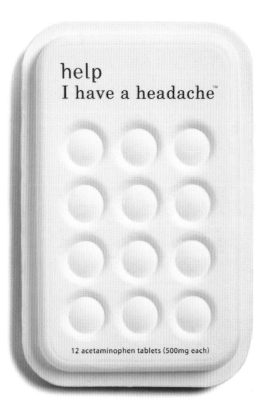

help
I have a headache™

12 acetaminophen tablets (500mg each)

As you can see, these pills have 500mg of
acetaminophen in them. They don't contain
Red Dye #40. If you enjoy Red Dye #40,
you will have to eat it separately.

Distributed by Help Remedies, New York, NY 10014
www.helpineedhelp.com
Lot 7K29096 Exp. 10/2010

Hello. I'm sorry about the headache. Don't be embarrassed.
It doesn't mean you are dim witted.
Maybe it means the opposite. Maybe
your thoughts are so radical they
have astounded your brain. You ought
to be proud of your headache.
"I have a headache," you should
say to your boss. "You're promoted,"
your boss will say.

But you probably want to get rid of
your headache. That's probably why
you purchased this package in the
first place. So sit down on a
pleasant object, and swallow two
tablets.

Help Remedies
New York, USA

As you can see, these pills have 500mg of
acetaminophen in them. They don't contain
Red Dye #40. If you enjoy Red Dye #40,
you will have to eat it separately.

Distributed by Help Remedies, New York, NY 10014
www.helpineedhelp.com
Lot 7K29096 Exp. 10/2010

Drug Facts

Active Ingredient (in each tablet) Purpose
Acetaminophen 500mg.......Analgesic/Antipyretic

Uses temporary relief of minor aches and pains
associated with • headache • common cold • toothache •
muscular aches • backache • arthritis • menstrual cramps

Warnings
Alcohol Warning: • If you consume 3 or more alcoholic
drinks every day, ask your doctor whether you should
take acetaminophen or other pain relievers/fever
reducers. • Acetaminophen may cause liver damage

Do not use • with other products containing acetaminophen

Stop use and ask a doctor if: • New symptoms occur
• Redness or swelling is present • Pain gets worse or
lasts for more than 10 days • Fever gets worse or lasts
for more than 3 days.

If pregnant or breast-feeding, ask a health professional
before use.

Keep out of reach of children. In case of accidental
overdose, contact a doctor or poison control center
immediately. Prompt medical attention is critical for adults
as well as for children even if you do not notice any signs
of symptoms. Do not exceed recommended dosage.

Directions
Adults & Children 12 years and over: Take 2 tablets every
4 to 6 hours as needed. Do not take more than 8 tablets
in 24 hours.Children under 12 years of age: Do not use
this extra strength product. This will provide more than
the recommended dose (overdose) and could cause
serious health problems.

Other Information • store at room temperature • do not
use if package has been tampered with

Inactive Ingredients corn starch, pregeletanized starch,
providone, sodium carboxymethylcellulose, stearic acid

Title
* Help I Have A Headache
** Help I've Cut Myself

Client
Help Remedies

Art Director
Little Fury, Chapps Malina

Graphic Designer
Little Fury

Structural Designer
Chapps Malina

Year Produced
2008

Description
Help Remedies was created to make solving simple health issues easy. Everything,
including the design, strips away some of the
complexity and fear mongering of the health
industry. Help Remedies hopes to make the
category friendlier and more accessible, and
in doing so to empowering people to make
their own health decisions. It is believed that
a little help, honesty and kindness would go
for a long way.

help
I've cut myself™

8 clear bandages. Two sizes

Don't be startled. The bandages inside don't look normal. That's because they are made of a futuristic material. It's the same material they use in hospitals. You can wear them for several days. Enjoy.

Distributed by Help Remedies, New York, NY 10014
www.helpineedhelp.com

Hello. I'm sorry you cut yourself. It could be an isolated incident, or maybe you are a very clumsy person. Don't worry. The clumsy are much more lovable than the graceful. The graceful are always busy ballet dancing, and doing incredible feats on the trapeze. The clumsy are always busy being coddled, rubbed, and cared for.

So if you're not too busy having attractive persons ravish you with affection, take a minute to care for your injury. Wash it, and lay one of our pretty bandages on top. In a matter of moments you will be able to return to your clumsy affairs.

Studio Kanna
Tokyo, Japan

Title
4Th_Floor Gift Box

Client
4Th_Floor

Art Director
Akiko Kanna

Designer
Akiko Kanna

Year Produced
2005

Description
The project was completed when Kanna worked at North.

Simply play with the number '4' which comes from the name of the company, 4TH_Floor. The company itself has a very simple and almost non-design identity because they believe that their products' quality can speak for themselves. Kanna wanted to create with a 3-dimensional approach, very simple but provides another view to their identity, when it's also playful at the same time. Each side of the box appears some parts of the number '4,' which creates various patterns when pile together.

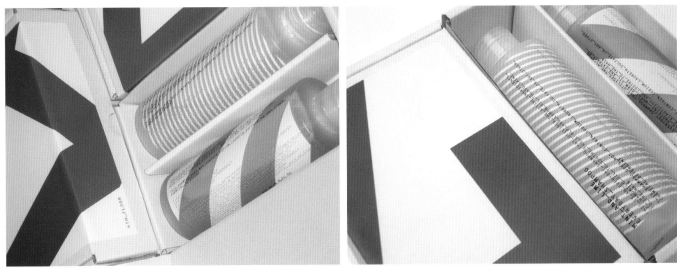

NONAME
NOSHOP
Seoul, Korea

Title
Take-out Garden

Client
'Seoul City Gallery Project,' Korea

Art Director
NONAME NOSHOP

Designer
NONAME NOSHOP

Year Produced
2007

Description
Take-out Garden is a paper cup with plant seeds in it. Take-out Garden Shop distributed paper cups to people who can then transplant the plants into the garden around the buildings when the plants grow.

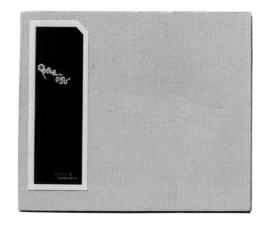

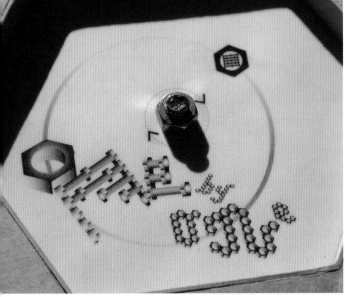

Maxime Delporte

Brussel, Belgium

Title
One by one

Client
Maxime Delporte

Art Director
Maxime Delporte

Designer
Maxime Delporte

Artist / Singer
Maxime Delporte

Year Produced
2006

Description
A fictitious company of sale and distribution of screw and bolts, One by one proposes an optimum service of reliability on their products with a system in which every single piece is controlled and counted one by one and each controller has a counting frame to avoid losing any single piece.

Different typographical systems are applied to increase the identity and the communication of the company. The abacus is used to count the bolts manually which are transformed into typographical matrices. On the other hand, the screws are used as pixel characters in varied assemblies. In this box, users can find the screws and bolts in kit form and use the used matrices to re-create the characters presented on the booklet or to seek for new ones. At the bottom of the box, users can find a CD with various fonts.

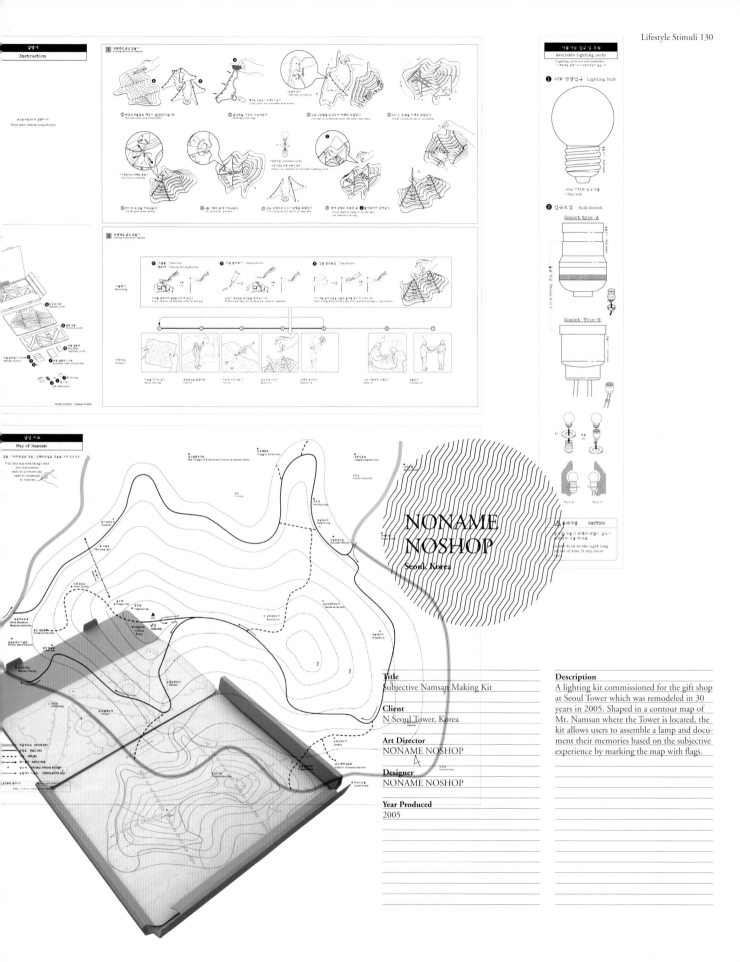

Title
Subjective Namsan Making Kit

Client
N Seoul Tower, Korea

Art Director
NONAME NOSHOP

Designer
NONAME NOSHOP

Year Produced
2005

Description
A lighting kit commissioned for the gift shop at Seoul Tower which was remodeled in 30 years in 2005. Shaped in a contour map of Mt. Namsan where the Tower is located, the kit allows users to assemble a lamp and document their memories based on the subjective experience by marking the map with flags.

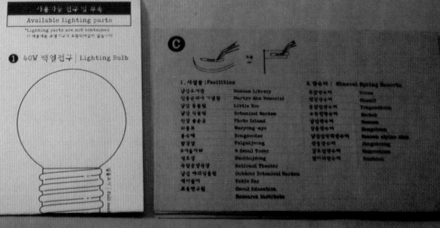

사용가능 전구및 부속
Available lighting parts
*Lighting parts are not contained

❶ 40W 백열전구 | Lighting Bulb

© 또는 or

1. 시설물 | Facilities

남산도서관	Namsan Library
안중근의사 기념관	Martyr Ahn Memorial
남산 동물원	Little Zoo
남산 식물원	Botanical Garden
사진 촬영도	Photo Island
와룡묘	Waryong-myo
봉수대	Bongsoodae
팔각정	Palgakjeong
N서울타워	N Seoul Tower
석호정	Smokhojeong
국립중앙극장	National Theater
남산 야외식물원	Outdoor Botanical Garden
케이블카	Cable Car
교육연구원	Seoul Education Research Institute

2. 약수터 | Mineral Spring Resorts

Ⓔ 꼬리 맞스 스티커 | Flag Sticker

N서울타워

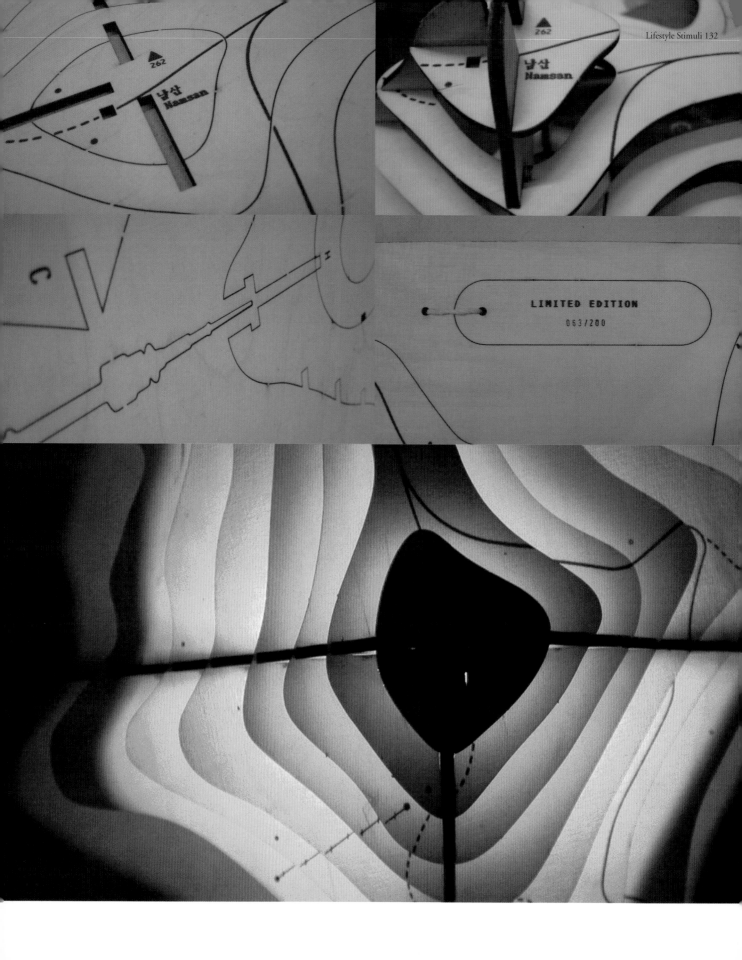

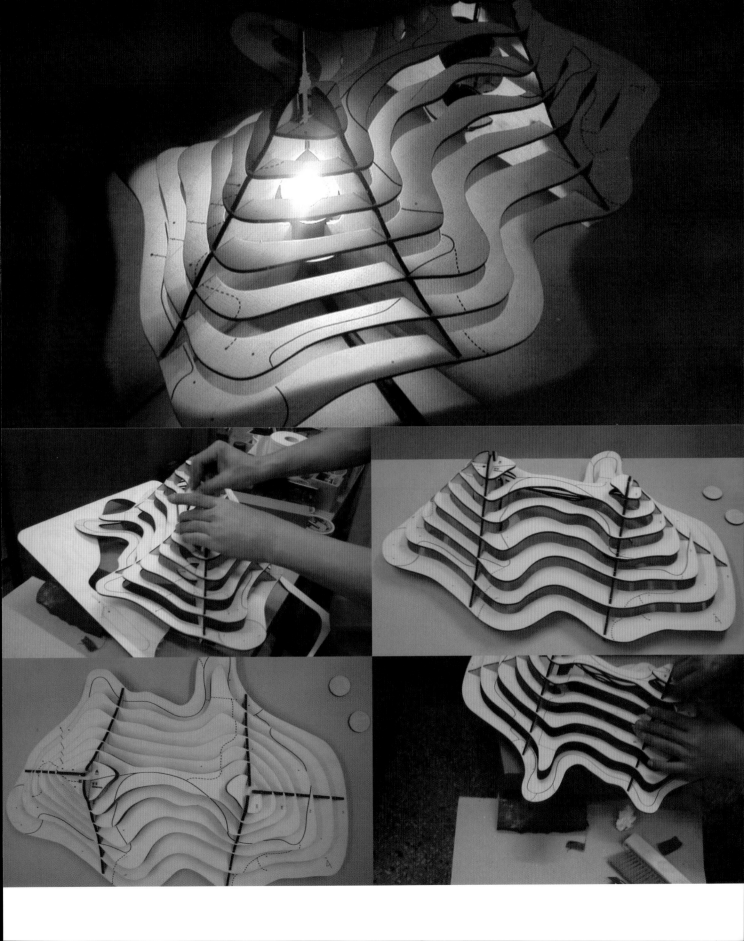

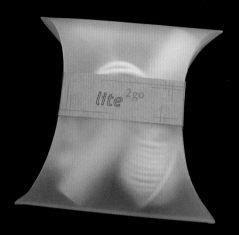

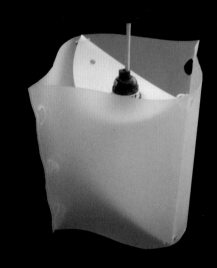

Knoend LLC
San Francisco, USA

Title
Lite2go

Client
Knoend

Designer
Ivy Chuang, Jane Rabanal, Anila Jain

Year Produced
2007

Description
Knoend's lite2go is a multi-functional lamp that eliminates packaging. This one-step, ready-to-use solution includes an electric cord and an energy-efficient compact florescent light bulb. The packaging itself becomes the shade for the light bulb and fixture contained within. It is designed to be versatile in use as either a hanging or a table lamp. The lite2go offers surprise and elegance in a simple, low-cost and lightweight package.

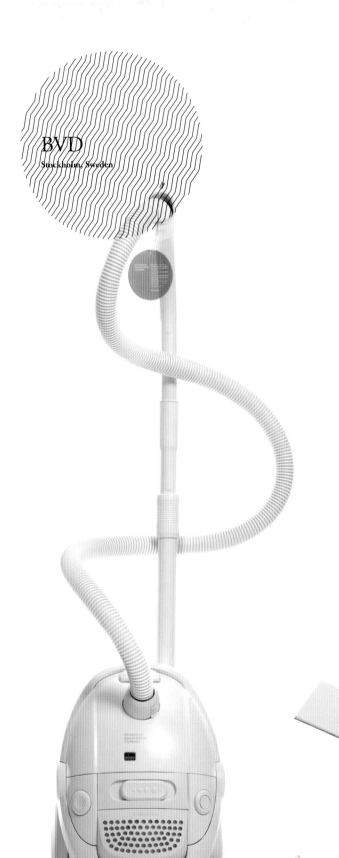

BVD
Stockholm, Sweden

Title
Ultrasilencer Special Edition Pia Wallén

Client
Electrolux Floor Care and Light Appliances

Creative Director
Susanna Nygren Barrett

Designer
Johan Andersson, Carolin Sundquist

Year Produced
2007

Description
The Ultrasilencer Special Edition Pia Wallén, one of the world's quietest vacuumcleaners, has now been introduced. The designer Pia Wallén was inspired by, among other things, silently falling snow, and the result is a completely white vacuum with accents in orange. BVD has translated Pia Wallén's design into a graphical expression to highlight the design and give it its own identity, name and packaging. The colours white, grey and orange were chosen to simplify the expression.

The graphic profile has been used on the vacuumcleaner, hangtags and promotional material. The packaging that BVD developed has an exterior in natural cardboard and a white, glossy interior closest to the product itself. A tote bag is also designed in recycled and new polyester that can be used later as a laundry bag and is included with the product.

The product is sold in a limited edition of only 5000 in Europe, with 500 on sale in Sweden. It is only available in the design store Asplunds and in Electrolux Home stores.

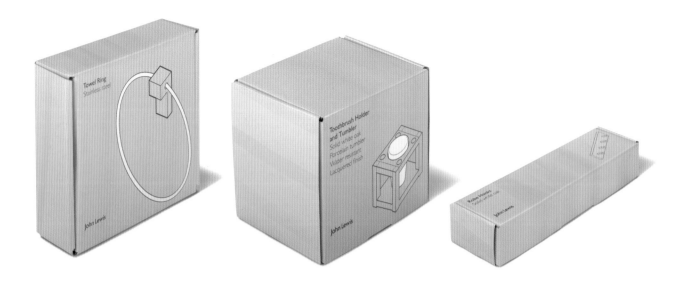

Dowling Design
& Art Direction
Nottinghamshire, UK

Title
John Lewis American White Oak Bathroom
Accessories

Client
John Lewis Partnership

Art Director
John McConnell, John Dowling

Designer
John Dowling

Year Produced
2007

Description
Commissioned to provide a packaging
solution for a range of American White Oak
bathroom accessories, the designers chose
to highlight the texture and colour of the
product. The grain of the wood has been
replicated on the surface of the packaging,
a UV spot varnish creates a slightly raised
finish. The colour of the American white oak
is consistent across a series of boxes designed
to feel solid and honest, like wood. Line
illustrations of products are punctuated by
elements highlighted in white – a graphic
device identifying elements (glasses, metal
towel rings etc.) made from materials other
than white oak.

Jesse Kirsch
New Jersey, USA

Title
Brand Generic Packaging

Client
Brand

Art Director
Jesse Kirsch

Designer
Jesse Kirsch

Year Produced
2006

Description
A direct, no-nonsense approach defines this line of generic store-brand packaging. Helvetica, grayscale colour palette, and newsprint-like stock were used in stark contrast to the rainbow of fancy, embossed and glossy packages that line the shelves at any supermarket. 'Brand' stands out from its competition by not standing out at all.

ANGLEPOISE®

Type3™ | Designed by Kenneth Grange
Made in England

Small
London, UK

***

**

Title
Product packaging (* Anglepoise Type75 task light ** Anglepoise Type3 task light)
*** Promotional poster and instructions leaflet for Anglepoise Type3 task light

Client
Anglepoise

Art Director
David Hitner, Guy Marshall

Designer
David Hitner, Guy Marshall

Year Produced
2006-07

Description
Anglepoise®, the original inventor of the spring balanced task light, has been plagued by poor imitations and over the years, their name has come to define a product category, like Kleenex and Hoover.

Part of Small's work to help re-establishing the Anglepoise® brand was to develop a strong graphic identity for all their products which follow through from initial promotion to final point of sale. Each new product is given its own graphic identity but still fits within the Anglepoise® family through the bold use of the product names and the strong silhouette the product makes.

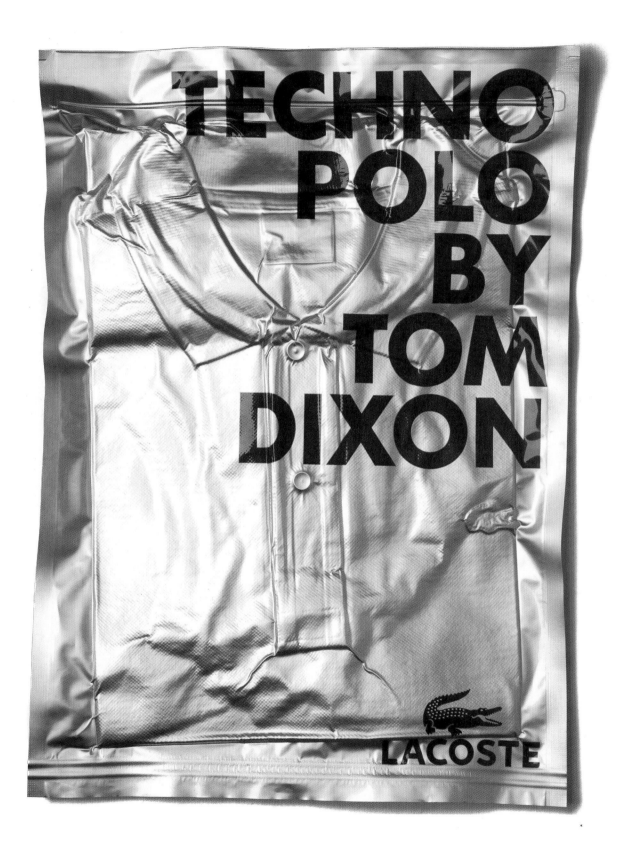

Tom Dixon
London, UK

Title	**Description**
* TECHNOPOLO ** ECOPOLO	Dixon was keen to explore two contrasting ideas for LACOSTE: one which engages in the provenance and craft of the materials used, and one that challenges the technology and functionality of the garment. The results are the ECOPOLO and the TECHNO-POLO.
Client	
LACOSTE	
Designer	* Continuing LACOSTE's heritage into the engineering of textiles for increased performance, Dixon chose to investigate the latest possibilities in yarn and post-production processes. The TECHNOPOLO combines hi-tech weaving of Lurex fibres and cotton to create a contemporary take on classic sportswear.
Tom Dixon	
Photographer	
Koichiro Matsui	
Year Produced	
2006	** In a world where mass production is ubiquitous, there is an increasing demand for the personal and the unique. Dixon was keen to explore this by using indigo dyes and organic cotton. This has produced the ECOPOLO, where every example is slightly different and unique.

*

**

Non-Format
London, UK

Title
LoAF Packaging

Client
LoAF / Lo Recordings

Art Director
Kjell Ekhorn, Jon Forss

Designer
Kjell Ekhorn, Jon Forss

Cover art print
* Yokoland ** Paul Winstanley
*** Ivan Zouravliov **** Ivan Zouravliov
***** Athanasios Argianas ****** Sergei
Sviatchenko ******* Manuel Schibli

Year Produced
2006-07

Description
3" or 5" CDs accompanied by art prints
by various artists and image-makers. Items
are enclosed in a sealed plastic documents
envelope attached to a 12" grey board cut
and then silkscreen overprinted with the
musician and artist names.

***

******

****

****

*****

Shya-la-la
Production Limited
Hong Kong, China

Title
Cavalulu

Client
Shya-la la Production Limited

Art Director
Wing Shya, Marcus Savage

Designer
Sarah Yung at Shya-la-la

Year Produced
2004

Description
Cava was born from a blow of the sun. Cava Lulu and Family's role is to use the rainbow tissue to wipe away the tears of people to bring joy to the world. Cava Lulu and Family each has a range of products from dolls to clothing apparels and fashionable accessories. Although developed in Hong Kong, the products are very popular and mainly sold in fashion boutiques in Japan.

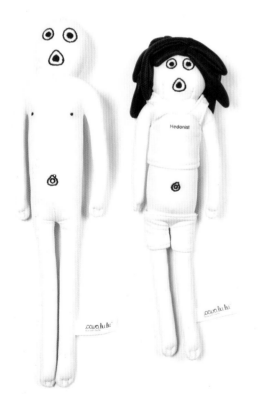

MOMENT
DESIGN STUDIO
Beijing, China

Title
MZ T-shirt

Client
MOMENT design studio

Art Director
Xiaoxue

Designer
Xiaoxue

Year Produced
2007

Description
Xiaoxue designed a line of six T-shirts, named MZ series, for the MOMENT design studio. Drawing inspiration from film, absurd theatricals and outer space, as well as his own childhood memories, he designed the line to also have a futuristic quality about it.

I am trying to exercise different visual languages in my work.
New visual context is created by merging and crashing
different visual languages. By looking at the internal
relationship between daily life and visual
elements, new experience will be revealed.
Movies, my childhood memory in 70s,
fantastic dramas, universe, future music and
etc often inspire my creativities.

www.2xd.com.cn

Kinetic
Singapore

Title
Concave Scream Horizons

Client
Concave Scream / EMI Singapore

Creative Director
Pann Lim, Roy Poh

Art Director
Leng Soh, Pann Lim, Roy Poh

Year Produced
2006

Description
This CD design was commissioned for a Singaporean band releasing their much-anticipated and long-overdue fourth album 'Horizons.' The entire packaging is designed to function as a calendar, this concept is intended to be a clear reference to the name 'Horizons,' which not only connotes the flow of time and the expectations towards the future, but also reflects the band's ongoing evolution towards a more mellow and contemplative sound.

As an additional touch, the liner notes and production information are printed via a special silkscreen process that will be gradually rubbed away with the wear and tear of use. Other than being a clear nod to the conceptual referencing of the unbreakable streams of time that bind us, the slow 'decay' that results from this 'biodegradable' printing also makes each and every one of the individual CD covers a living and breathing art piece.

JOYN:VISCOM
Beijing, China

Title
Nike Air Max360 LX

Client
Nike

Art Director
Wei Xingyu

Designer
Wei Xingyu

Year Produced
2006

Description
The design was mainly based on the two ideas 360 visible and max air behind the product Nike Air Max360 LX. The best juncture between these two characteristics was the air cushion, which is commonly used in packaging to reduce the shock, that contains similar concepts with the shoes. PVC was the key material in the package design, it would come into a box after charging.

The logo design is a combination of Liu Xiang, the Olympic gold medal winner, and the flaming wings image with the 4 Chinese characters, which conveys his speed and overall charisma.

Checkland
Kindleysides
Leicestershire, UK

Title
Speedo Fastskin Packaging

Client
Speedo

Designer
Checkland Kindleysides

Year Produced
2002

Description
Whilst the skin of the shark was the inspiration for the fabric of the Speedo Fastskin suit; it was the shark's egg that inspired the packaging design.

A net pouch allows the suit to be compressed into its smallest form and doubled as a quick dry bag.

A tactile, semi-translucent pouch contains this 'net' and printed / embossed graphics subtly branded the packaging.

Nikki Farquharson
London, UK

Title
All Wrapped Up – The Best Jackets of the
Decade

Client
Nikki Farquharson (Self-initiated project)

Designer
Nikki Farquharson

Year Produced
2007

Description
The brief was to create a jacket for a book
titled All Wrapped Up that would hold the
best book jackets from the past decade. Although the book was fictional, Farquharson
thought it was important not to compete
with the jackets that were to exist within
the pages. She used the title of the book and
the bookmark ribbon as inspiration instead.
Using extremely long ribbons, Farquharson
continually wrapped the cover while weaving
on the front and back. This created a simple
pattern for the cover, which does not distract
or compete with the jackets inside.

Michael Young Ltd
Hong Kong, China

Title
Lacoste Plastic Polo

Client
Lacoste

Designer
Michael Young

Year Produced
2007

Description
Years ago Young discovered these colourful gardening gloves in Japan that had a latex coating and started collecting them, but until now he never found any use for them. Plastic has always been his favorite material, and for LACOSTE, Young wanted to experiment with combining plastics and fabrics to create a fresh, futuristic polo that reflects the heritage of the brand. It was also a great challenge as a product and interior designer used to working with hard surfaces to be faced with soft, flexible fabrics.

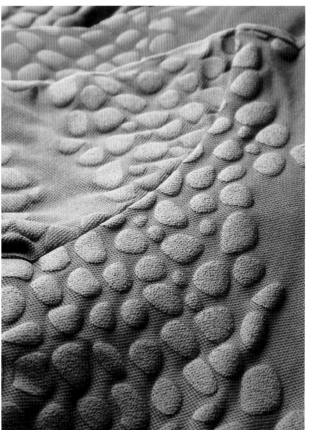

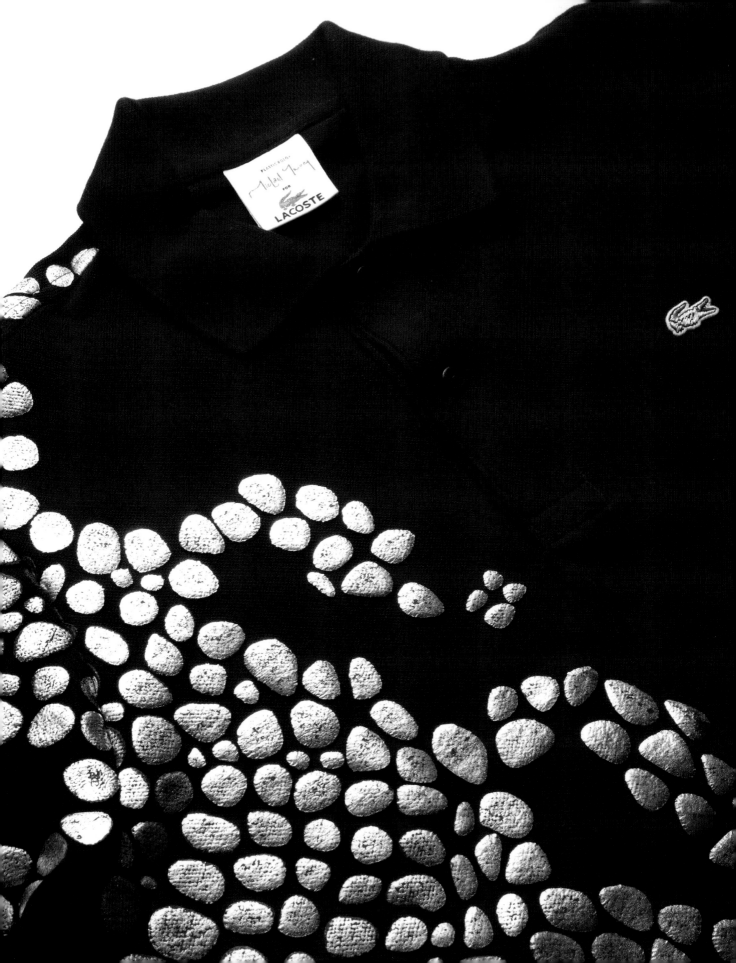

Title
Dog Poo Bags

Client
jungeschachtel

Art Director
Andrea Gadesmann, Nina Dautzenberg

Designer
Andrea Gadesmann, Nina Dautzenberg

Year Produced
2008

Description
Dog Poo Bags are humorous paper bags for the stylish and practical disposal of dog poo. They turn the less attractive moments in the life of a dog owner into an original happening. 16 recyclable paper bags come in one size mean a simple, clean and practical disposal of dog poo. Funny prints, such as 'Doggy bag,' 'Don't blame me' or 'Size matters' make the walk to the next garbage bin an easy task.

It's an ultimate gift for cosmopolitan dog lovers. A stylish accessory that fits easily into every bag. A humorous call on other dog owners to dispose of nasty dog poo in an elegant way. It is designed for all races from Chihuahua to Great Dane.

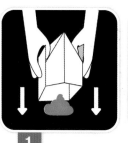

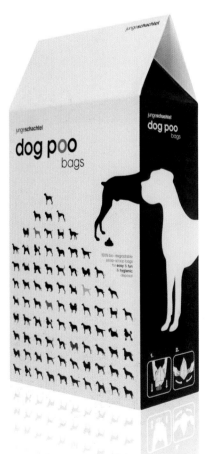

aruliden
New York, USA

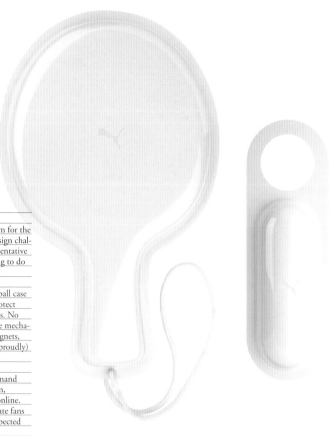

Title
PUMA PT3 Ultramagnetic Collection

Client
PUMA

Art Director
Johan Liden, Rinat Aruh

Designer
Johan Liden

Graphic Designer
Tyler Askew

Photographer
Dustin Ross

Year Produced
2007

Description
Puma wanted to create an iconic item for the passionate sport, ping pong. The design challenge was to create something representative of the PUMA brand, yet had nothing to do with their core product directly.

The PUMA ping pong paddle-and-ball case is a simple and iconic solution to protect and carry ping pong paddle and balls. No zippers, no buttons, no hard-to-close mechanisms, and enclosed simply with magnets, the case enables users to easily (and proudly) access their ping pong equipment.

The project resulted in extensive demand for the PT3 Ultramagnetic collection, with requests at the retail level and online. Ultimately, it allowed PUMA to create fans out of their customers with an unexpected design object.

Dowling Design
& Art Direction
Nottinghamshire, UK

Title
Simon Patterson Colour Match Screensaver

Client
Tate Modern

Art Director
John Dowling

Designer
John Dowling

Year Produced
2001

Description
Turner Prize-nominated artist Simon Patterson has created three works in his 'Colour Match' series, all with packaging designed by Dowling Design & Art Direction. The third work in the series is a screensaver featuring a recording of football commentator John Cavanagh reading football results: Pantone colours and their codes represent teams and goals, and the results are announced with different Pantone colours filling the screen. The CD's packaging – a foam football held in a net bag (both ball and net in blue or red), echoes the subject matter. A booklet of instructions for installing the CD is attached to the net.

gobbling desire
gulzige verleiding
engullimiento de deseo
垂涎的衝動
デザイン×欲求
먹는 것에 대한 욕망

From traditional whiskey to organic juices, from gourmet
pastries to sushi take-aways, this chapter is a selection
of the finest in food and beverage packaging, witnessing
how typography, colour, material and creative structural
packaging are utilised to communicate the brand
and bring out the product's essence to appeal to one's
exquisite taste.

SEED Creative
Consultants
London, UK & Singapore

Title
Wild Bunch & Co. Organic Juice

Client
Wild Bunch & Co. Organic Juice

Designer
Mark Walker, Garnet Teo

Year Produced
2007-08

Description
The objective was to design a range of
packaging that signaled the inherent value of
the organic product WB&CO (Wild Bunch
& Co.) used in all its juice and their respect
for it. To do this, the designers chose to use
glass as the material for the bottles, which
could clearly show customers the vibrant
colours of the vegetable juice that naturally
speaks for itself . The colour shows the
importance of WB&CO's organic products
as they are made without artificial additives.

Additionally, as required in the brief, the
pure and simple design of the bottles
is 100% refillable. It allows customers
to exchange their empty bottles at local
WB&CO Organic Shot Bars.

BVD
Stockholm, Sweden

Title
Candyking

Client
Candyking International Ltd.

Art Director
Rikard Ahlberg

Designer
Bengt Anderung

Year Produced
2005

Description
The previous identity of Candyking was unclear, and looked old-fashioned and outdated. BVD was asked to strengthen the brand and make it more of a present in-store with a new corporate identity in all communication units.

The new corporate identity was required to appeal to adults and children, and to be simple, unique and strong enough to establish the brand as a category leader in an otherwise 'unbranded' sector. Candyking was also looking to launch in the international market.

BVD created the 'Candyking's kingdom,' from which all communication would emanate. The king himself was given a more contemporary appearance and a friendlier personality while the colours convey joy and variety.

Launched in autumn 2006, the new identity has been well presented everywhere, and has strengthened Candyking's position in the Pick & Mix market.

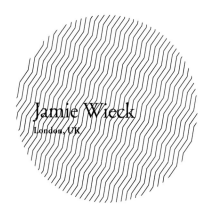

Jamie Wieck
London, UK

Title
Say It With Chocolate

Client
Jamie Wieck (Self-initiated project)

Art Director
Jamie Wieck

Designer
Jamie Wieck

Year Produced
2006

Description
'Say It With Chocolate' was an idea to create an insulated chocolate box that would melt its contents, printing a design onto its inner lid during transit. With this in mind, Wieck designed a heavily insulated box along with a double-sided chocolate that would allow the sender to lay out a message surprising the recipient.

The chocolates have a very low melting point, so even room temperature can cause a print. Flat on one side and concave on the other, the chocolate is capable of printing either a ring or a circle depending on how it's placed - giving meaning to the phrase 'saying it with chocolate.'

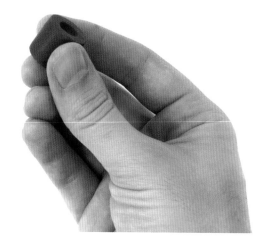

SAY IT WITH CHOCOLATE

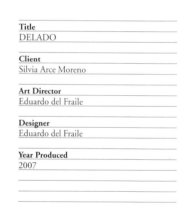

DFraile
Madrid, Spain

Title
DELADO

Client
Silvia Arce Moreno

Art Director
Eduardo del Fraile

Designer
Eduardo del Fraile

Year Produced
2007

Description
DELADO is a pun implying both helado
(ice cream) and sideways (de lado).

The identity is designed for an ice-cream
parlour located in a corner of a central
quarter of the city. It consists of special
typography and an image of old ice-cream
wafer with chequered reticule.

Naoto Fukasawa
Tokyo, Japan

Title
Juice skin

Client
TAKEO PAPER SHOW 2004 'HAPTIC'

Designer
Naoto Fukasawa

Year Produced
2004

Description
An obtuse eight-faceted Tetra juice pack – Its chilly feeling, along with the weight on the juice contained within, overlapped with the sensations one gleans from a banana. The bruises on its rounded obtuse angles, and the change from yellow to green at the end of the banana's stalk overlapped with the shape of the folded-over part at the top of the package. The package was named 'Juice skin' as the moisture between both the juice and the fruit enclosed in a skin. This design was displayed at the Haptic exhibition.

Michael Young
Ltd
Hong Kong, China

Title
Nikka Whisky Bottle

Client
Nikka Whisky

Art Director
Michael Young

Designer
Michael Young

Year Produced
2007

Description
The Nikka Whisky bottle is made of glass, and the intention of the design is to enrich the whiskey bottle market. This is a prototype of the bottle.

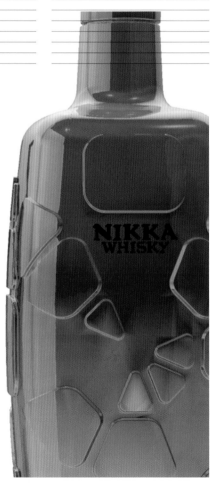

Little Fury

New York, USA

Title
Bee Hive Honey

Client
BeeHive

Art Director
Esther Mun

Designer
Esther Mun

Year Produced
2001

Description
BeeHive Honey takes inspiration from bees collecting honey. The clear honey frame containers allow consumers to see and appreciate the beautiful and pure natural colours of different kinds of honey. The familiar wooden box used by the bee keepers, is also used in the package as a wooden case that holds all the clear frames together. The BeeHive identity is based around the simple idea of love for honey, which is reflected through the incorporation of the honey comb with the shape of a heart.

Waldo Pancake
London, UK

Title
Puccino's identity

Client
Puccino's

Art Director
Jim Smith

Designer
Jim Smith

Year Produced
2001-08

Description
Smith hopes the people who gets his design would like to cuddle it and say, 'Don't worry, you'll be alright now.'

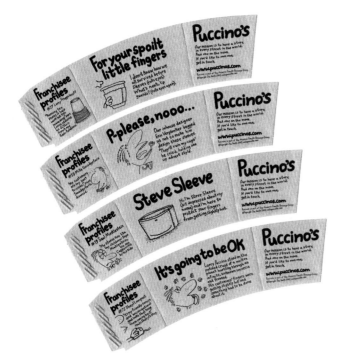

DISPOSE OF POSTMODERN-IRONICALLY.

Carrying stuff around is the new leaving it where it is.

Puccino's

Cappuccino. Proven to reverse the recede.*

Puccino's

use as very small pillow.

WHITE BROWN OTHER

Ingredients: sugar, and then some.

NO KNEE BOBBING
(IT'S ANNOYING.)

Dimaquina
Rio de Janeiro - RJ, Brazil

Title
Popfish

Client
Popfish

Art Director
Dimaquina, Giosimi

Designer
Daniel Neves at Dimaquina,
João Simi at Giosimi

Year Produced
2008

Description
Popfish is a restaurant / shop located in
Rio de Janeiro. The design was inspired
by Japanese and Tokyo imagery, using
illustrations and characters to enhace its
visual identity. A highlight in the visual
identity project is that each Popfish shop has
a theme colour added to the shop's name.
The first one is called Popfish Magenta.
More than a restaurant, Popfish is an
attempt to join gastronomy and design at
the same spot.

C plus C
Workshop Ltd.
Hong Kong, China

Title
Cake With Care

Client
Baking Warehouse LTD.

Art Director
C plus C Workshop

Year Produced
2005

Description
The idea of Cake With Care comes from 'handle with care,' a message always catches consumer's attention. It is made to improve life with enjoyment, mainly through its package and boxes. And to do this, stylish and modern illustrations have been used to arouse fun and happiness for consumers.

CAKE WITH CARE

No matter whether you are a bakery lover or dieter, enjoy the pastry which can bring you happiness at all time and feel the swing! Remember this precious memory and share the happy moment with all your family and friends.

CHOCOLATE WITH CARE

No matter whether you are a bakery lover or dieter, enjoy the pastry which can bring you happiness at all time and feel the swing! Remember this precious memory and share the happy moment with all your family and friends.

Designworks
Victoria, Australia

Title
VISY Closed Loop - The Enviro Range

Client
VISY Closed Loop

Art Director
Serena Cheung

Designer
Tim Harding

Year Produced
2007

Description
The VISY Closed Loop Enviro Range is a product with high quality recyclable packaging using the Closed Loop recycling program, which collects used packs and re-manufactures them into new end use products, maximising landfill diversion and environmental benefits.

The brief called for a typographic solution that explored the Enviro Ranges key features. The concept of juxtaposing lines from pop songs with the key objectives and features of the packaging, such as recycling, recycled materials, collection, sorting and reusing. These popular culture references the increase of the connection as well as the recall of the packaging, message and the brand.

Carlo Giovani
Studio
São Paulo, Brazil

Title	Description
* Chinese Tea Box ** Packagepeople	* It's a self-initiated project of gifts for clients. The Chinese Tea Box is part of a project that seeks to create new concepts for some ordinary packaging we use every day, giving users some new faces or creating characters to represent the element into the box, in fact, creating a kind of a 'toy-packs.' The idea is to make consumers keep it after use and reuse it for other purposes.

Client
* Carlo Giovani Studio
** Capricho Magazine

Editor
* Carlo Giovani ** Alceu Nunes

Illustrator / Photographer
* Carlo Giovani ** Carlo Giovani

** The Packagepeope is a character project. The idea was to make some typical persons in a pack shape.

Year Produced
2006

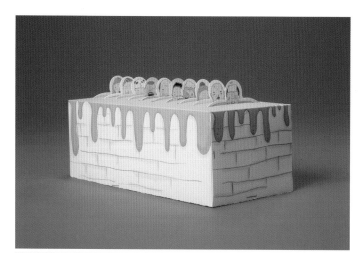

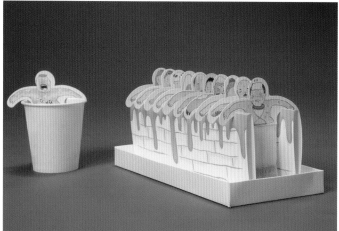

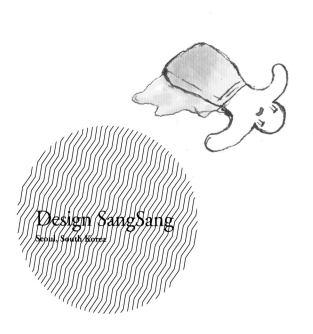

Design SangSang
Seoul, South Korea

Title
Maum (Warmer Warmer Tea)

Client
Wdaru (Self-initiated project)

Art Director
Lee Dal-woo

Designer
Tuna, Lee Dal-woo

Year Produced
2007

Description
Disposable tea bag series designed for hard job workers who are under stress. Everyday, many people use tea bags and just throw it away after use, the designers find it very wasteful. Nice graphics with little cute figures resting in bath is put on the front of the tea bags while spaces are provided at the back for writing up messages. This warm-hearted tea bag could give people a chance to smile during teatime.

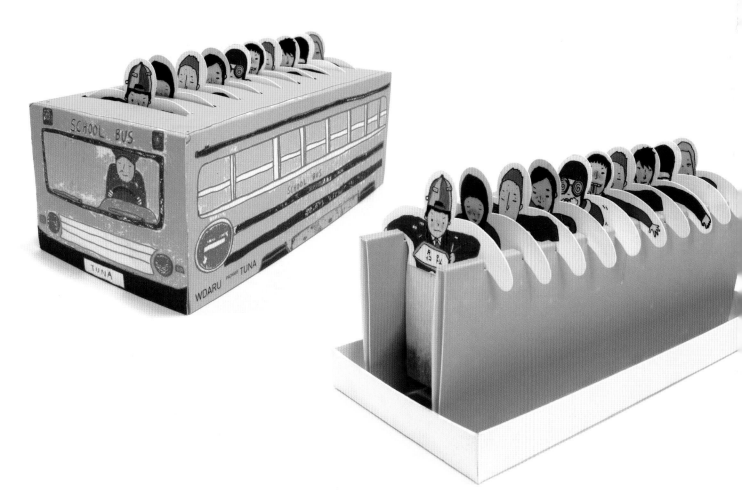

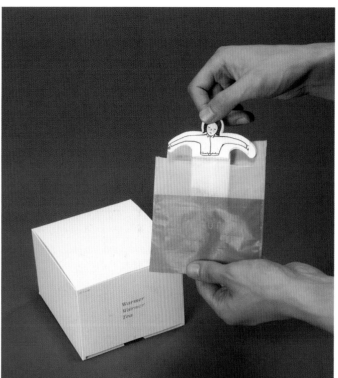

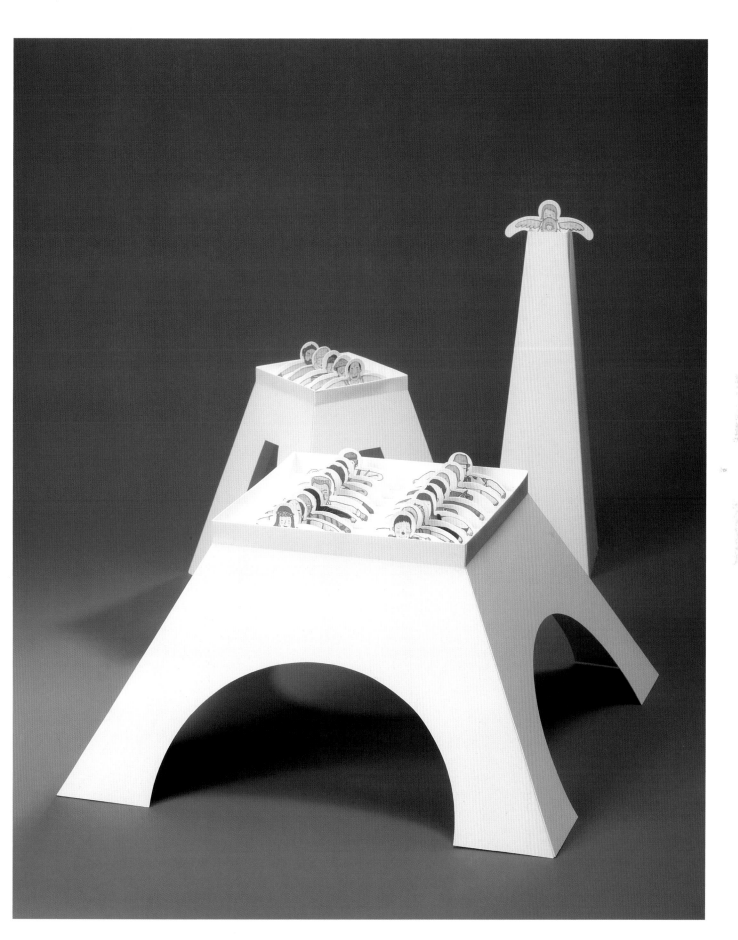

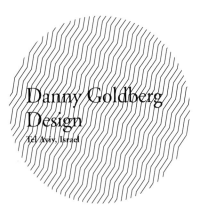

Danny Goldberg
Design
Tel Aviv, Israel

Title
Cérémonie

Client
Cérémonie Tea

Art Director
Danny Goldberg

Designer
Danny Goldberg

Year Produced
2004

Description
A complete identity development for an international boutique tea product line. Defining its concept, language, logo and packaging, the visual language combines the elements of the traditional Japanese tea ceremony, with Western elegance and prestige.

Megan Cummins
Georgia, USA

Title
Doggybag Bakery

Client
Doggybag Bakery

Art Director
Megan Cummins

Designer
Megan Cummins

Year Produced
2008

Description
Doggybag Bakery was created for the pampered pooch. It is said that every dog has its day, but we believe that everyday should be a special day for your four-legged friend. Our furry friends should enjoy the full experience of gourmet dining just as we do, from presentation to taste.

Here at Doggybag Bakery, ingredients was made to be safe for canine consumption, yet every bit as delicious as a treat slipped to them, under the dinning table. Every dog is unique which should be pampered with special food.

238 Cupcake Ln. Soho, NY 18318

doggybag bakery

238 Cupcake Ln. Soho, NY 18318

Marque
London, UK & New York, USA

Title
Kshocolât

Client
Kshocolât

Art Director
Mark Noe

Designer
Marque

Year Produced
2006-07

Description
Kshocolât is a Scotland-based company that manufactures luxury handmade chocolates. Marque was appointed to create and consolidate the brand, which would differentiate its product from other elite, specialised chocolate companies, and position it at the high-end consumer market. Refined typography, sophisticated colour palette, hand-tipped labels, self-coloured uncoated slip covers and brushed aluminium tins have all strengthened the simplistic design and reflected the quality and luxury of the product. With over 50 items, from lemon and pepper to orange and cardamom, each product has been carefully considered.

BVD
Stockholm, Sweden

Title
Stories

Client
Turesgruppen

Creative Director
Susanna Nygren Barrett

Designer
Johan Andersson

Year Produced
2006-07

Description
Stories Götgatan was opened in November 2007. A project of Turesgruppen, which already owns a number of cafés and restaurants in Stockholm, is a new café concept developed by BVD in cooperation with Ivan Akibar Arkitekter. Housed in the newly opened mall, Skrapan, cafés in each neighbourhood and city looks different but with same feeling.

BVD wanted to create a conscious, mature, inviting and personal environment. Black and white stainless steel is blended with warm wood in a feeling of old fashioned café expressed by things such as a board with old, detachable letters and traditional cups and trays. The design is made to exude quality, style and a hip big city feeling with clean and simple graphics, but surprising and playful at the same time. Everything from porcelain to little packets of sugar can be found there.

Amore
Stockholm, Sweden

Title
BeB

Client
Bonden Butik

Art Director
Jörgen Olofsson

Designer
Sarah Ringquist

Year Produced
2005

Description
With the non-siding colour black, Amore developed a dynamic identity for this grass-root food store chain. BeB, a farmers' indoor market, aims to attract a growing number of young consumers who are impatient to the dominant supermarket chains. Amore helped with the development of in-store concept, visual identity, naming and logotype design.

Homework
Copenhagen K, Denmark

Title
TastePlease

Client
TastePlease

Designer
Jack Dahl

Year Produced
2006-07

Description
TastePlease® is an organic food market for everyone who wants to enjoy good food everyday, from organic bread of their own bakery, to takeaway delicacies, creative cakes, homemade soft drinks, easy food and specialities from all over the world.

At TastePlease, consumers can try a bite of Ecuador, savour the fragrance of Italy's sophisticated cuisine or enjoy the natural taste of homemade crisps from England's smallest crisp manufacturer. TastePlease can also tempt consumers with local specialities such as homemade nettle biscuits or cheeses from small dairies around Denmark. TastePlease has been developed out of a passion for good food based on respect for the environment, which is why Homework only uses biodegradable packaging for their food.

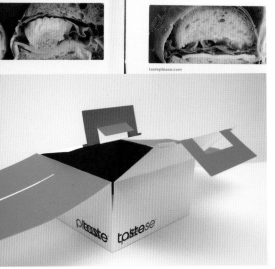

H55
Singapore

Title
The Sandwich Shop Packaging

Client
The Sandwich Shop

Art Director
Hanson Ho, Brenda Ng

Designer
Hanson Ho

Year Produced
2003

Description
The Sandwich Shop required a packaging design that reveals their various types of customised breads as well as their generous all-round sandwich fillings, in an attempt to attract customers to try out their various recipes.

H55's custom moulded plastic packaging allows customers to get a clear all-round view of the sandwiches. A slide-and-remove backing card acts as a vehicle for communication, highlighting The Sandwich Shop's beliefs and values.

The packaging also contains a 'freebie' (normally in the form of a cherry tomato or a lime), and a stand which doubles up as a 'finger slot' for customers to sink their fingers in to lift up their sandwiches.

dävid cheung

the sändwich shop
no.61 robinson road
robinson centre
unit number 01-02
singapore 068893
t : +65 65365 232
f : +65 65365 282
m: +65 98323 647
e : ahbcheung@hotmail.com

denny lim

the sändwich shop
no.61 robinson road
robinson centre
unit number 01-02
singapore 068893
t : +65 65365 232
f : +65 65365 282
m: +65 97965 662
e : dennylam@hotmail.com

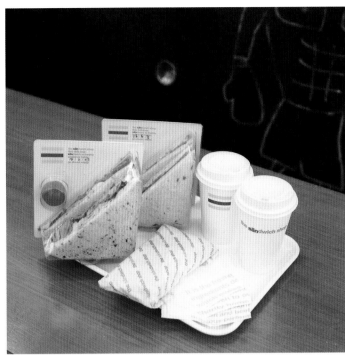

The Creative Method
Sydney, Australia

Title
Guzman Y Gomez Brand Identity

Client
Guzman Y Gomez

Art Director
Tony Ibbotson

Designer
Tony Ibbotson

Photographers & Illustrators
Mark Callanan, Tony Ibbotson,
Ashley Mackevicius, Watermark

Year Produced
2006

Description
Takeaway Mexican cuisine is taking the Australian market by storm. With its healthy low fat content of fresh ingredients, unique spices and flavours, it is set to revolutionise the quality of takeaway food.

The brandmark has been based on a sun with rays of light shining through the hero characters just like they have been blessed by the almighty. When developing the GYG logo, the designer specially designed and built an original typeface based on adhesive tape that the company could own. Elements such as menus, packaging, etc. are produced on uncoated stock to give it a more 'street feel.'

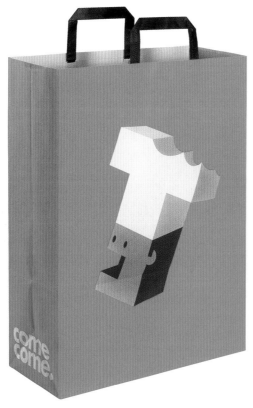

DFraile
Madrid, Spain

Title
ComeCome

Client
ComeCome

Art Director
Eduardo del Fraile

Designer
Eduardo del Fraile, Juan Jimenez,
David Racci

Year Produced
2006

Description
The image is based on elements and people
involved in the pizza place. The pizza place
is linked to the name and the concept that
everything from furniture to paper bags
and chef figures looks mouth-watering to
customers.

**manual
de buenas
prácticas
en locales**
comecome

evita incluir
al cocinero como
parte del menú.
un cocinero maduro
es garantía de confianza.

si eres un bombón
acepta los piropos.
o formarás parte
del postre.

vigila animales
de compañía
próximos
a comecome.
no toda la desmotivable
es comestible.

si escribes con
la boca abierta,
no confundas el cubierto.

el diseño de
nuestros locales
es exquisito,
para no hacemos cotas.

come
come.

una pizza
comecome.

Williams
Murray Hamm
London, UK

Title
Sainsburys Organic

Client
Sainsburys

Art Director
Garrick Hamm

Designer
Grant Willis

Year Produced
2005

Description
Sainsburys actively locates more locally grown British organic food than any other retailer. The challenge was to give the range a very particular Sainsbury's spin in order to become a credible and lead player in organic retail food. The solution actively works on transparency, exposing how each of the products is grown for Sainsbury's.

Each pack shows a sapling or branch from roots to tips. To give more credibility, the range moves from 'Organics' to 'Sainsbury's So Organics' giving brand definition and ownership over competitors. Each image is a shot on a natural and earthy green background supported by short written anecdotes, which delivers an unique story behind each product or its dedicated farmers.

Hatch Design
San Francisco, USA

Title
* Fuelosophy ** Coca-Cola Holiday 07

Client
* Pepsi Cola ** Coca-Cola

Art Director
* Joel Templin ** Joel Templin, Katie Jain

Designer
* Katie Jain ** Ryan Meis

Year Produced
2007

Description
* Pepsi brought Hatch Design on board to help them venture into the natural foods category with their first natural and healthy energy drink, Fuelosophy. Hatch Design created the Fuelosophy brand and packaging, with its handcrafted logo and simple layout, to be distinctively different from Pepsi's regular mainstream grocery brands and appeal to the more premium natural-foods shopper.

** For Holiday 2007, Coca-Cola appointed Hatch Design to create a graphic and iconic Holiday campaign for their five largest brands (Coca-Cola Classic, Diet Coke, Coca-Cola Zero, Sprite and Fanta). The illustrations Hatch Design created represent the individual character of each brand and also work together in a system to communicate the 'Give, Live, Love' holiday message.

Amore
Stockholm, Sweden

Title
* LLL ** Cider

Client
Krönleins Bryggeri

Art Director
Jörgen Olofsson

Designer
Håkan Schallinger

Year Produced
* 2004 ** 2003

Description
* Krönleins Brewery wanted a new, unexpected beer for the trendy urbanite. Amore developed LLL, means 'little light lager,' slick enough for anyone who wants to keep them cool. LLL won Bronze in EPICA 2005.

** The low-cost cider needed a brand position powerful enough to establish itself in the competitive cider market. Second and fourth on the sales lists in Sweden, the cider cans' distinctive identity won gold at the European advertising and design competition EPICA. Without any additional marketing efforts, Cider is planned to be sold in the Norwegian, Italian and German markets.

Ryszard Bienert

Poznan, Poland

Title
Paints project

Client
Astra

Art Director
Ryszard Bienert

Designer
Ryszard Bienert

Year Produced
2006

Description
Two designs for acrylic paints, mainly focused on the colour name and catalogue code number.

Jesse Kirsch
New Jersey, USA

Title
Deep Water

Client
Deep Water

Art Director
Jesse Kirsch

Designer
Jesse Kirsch

Year Produced
2007

Description
Elegant and clean typography along with the unique caddy design allows Deep Water to stand out from the crowd. The large white letters of 'DEEP' along with small droplet in pale blue allow the clear water inside the bottle looks prominent and appetizing. The caddy, featuring a self-holding joint, needs only a small sticker on the other end to remain closed. The sticker not only acts as a means to keep the caddy closed, but also serves as its label printed with a barcode, price and other information. Two small notches in the caddy allow the customer to hold the 4-pack comfortably.

Title
Water Bottle for Hotel Mukayu

Client
Beniya Mukayu

Art Director
Kenya Hara

Designer
Kenya Hara

Year Produced
2003

Description
A water bottle designed for Beniya Mukayu, a hotel in Kanazawa. The water is served and sold to guests who stay at the hotel.

Nippon Design
Center, Inc.
Tokyo, Japan

Title
Package design for Hakkin

Client
Masuichi-Ichimura Sake Brewery

Art Director
Kenya Hara

Designer
Kenya Hara

Year Produced
2000

Description
Bottle design for 'Hakkin Sake,' produced by Masuichi Ichimura Sake Brewery in Obuse-do, Nagano Prefecture, the mirror-like material of the bottle makes it looks disappearing in its environment.

Nippon Design
Center, Inc.
Tokyo, Japan

Nippon Design Center, Inc.
Tokyo, Japan

Title
* Bottle design for Grace Koshu
** Package for Dandelion Wine

Client
* Grace Winery Co., Ltd.
** Mukawa, Hokkaido

Art Director
Kenya Hara

Designer
* Rie Shimoda ** Kenya Hara

Year Produced
1999

Description
* There are only a few internationally ac-credited wineries in Japan. The Grace Wine Chuo Budoshu in Yamanashi Prefecture is one of them. There is an extremely clear wine description in Japanese on the label.

** The 'Tampopo (Dandelion) sake' is spe-cially produced in the village of Tsurukawa-cho, Japan's northern island of Hokkaido, where the largest number of dandelions in Japan is found. On the label, there is an etching of the plumed seeds of dandelion, which count grows one by one every year.

espluga+associates
Barcelona, Spain

*

Title
* Estrella Levante
** Damm Monoblock project

Client
Damm

Art Director
espluga+associates

Designer
espluga+associates

Year Produced
* 2006 ** 2005

Description
* Design of the monoblock bottle for the special edition of the Estrella Levante beer, the brief required to include concepts of night, diversity, and modernity. The pack was launched with a very powerful buzz marketing campaign with the theme, 'the secret.' The bottle was designed to carry the theme in a subtle way as it would remain in the market after the campaign finished.

** It's a packaging design competition for a special edition of the Spain's best selling beer company. The brief required to include the theme of 'night' and 'trend/coolness.' For that, the designers developed 3 different approaches: 'the bottle as the media,' 'the bottle is a message,' and 'the bottle looks cool.'

**

BVD
Stockholm, Sweden

Title
Blossa Annual Edition

Client
V&S Group

Art Director
BVD

Designer
BVD

Year Produced
1993

Description
BLOSSA årgångsglögg is an important member of the BLOSSA family. The aim of the vintage mulled wine is made to generate awareness of BLOSSA ahead of the mulled wine season and drive sales across the whole range. The design needs to capture the essence of the year's flavour and be unique and alluring.

The bottle is made shorter and rounder than other BLOSSA products. The shape of the bottle is kept from year to year, with the colours and typography changing to reflect that particular year's design and flavour. The design and the flavours have helped generating major publicity for the product every year.

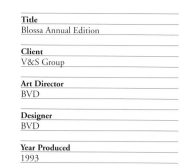

DFraile
Madrid, Spain

Title
O de Oliva

Client
Export Olive Oil

Art Director
Eduardo del Fraile

Designer
Eduardo del Fraile

Year Produced
2006

Description
Aimed at the European market and looking for consumers concerned about the manufacturing process and the quality of oil, O de Oliva is included in the range of products bearing an environmental certificate. It can accurately reflect how beneficial it is for people's health.

By choosing a pack from the pharmaceutical market, it is implied that the product is beneficial for people's health. In order to preserve the quality of the oil, DFraile used an opaque coloured bottle. To place the bottle as a point of reference in the environmentally friendly market, both client and DFraile prefer a minimal design that shows its purity of content.

Mash
Adelaide, Australia

Title
Mollydooker Packaging

Client
Mollydooker

Art Director
Dom Roberts, James Brown

Designer
Dom Roberts, James Brown

Year Produced
2006

Description
To reinforce the brand identity, Mash created the packaging that in no way reflected from any of their competitors and to make it stand out from the crowd communicating the hands-on approach that the wine makers take in producing their wines. Printed on a thick uncoated paper stock, the labels were created entirely from hand-drawn illustrations to the use of hand-drawn typeface, not a single font in sight, which were inspired by antique book patterns and 1930s advertising and cartoon illustrations.

The Partners.
London, UK

Title
Casa Loreto

Client
Jean Fraser-Cami

Creative Chairman
Aziz Cami

Creative Director
Nina Jenkins

Designer
Robert Young

Placement
Meeta Chauhan

Production Managers
Kathy Crawford, Tracey Martin

Year Produced
2006

Description
This premium olive oil from Casa Loreto in Tuscany is considered to be of such high quality that it is known as 'oro liquido,' or 'liquid gold.' This was the inspiration for the design solution. A simple and elegant three-dimensional golden drip gliding down the front of the bottle is made in contrast to the over complicated norm in a saturated product market.

Casa Loreto

**Oro liquido
Olio Extravergine
di Oliva**

Olio d'oliva di categoria superiore ottenuto direttamente dalle olive e unicamente mediante procedimenti meccanici.

Studio Copyright
Barcelona, Spain

Title
Mas Romaní

Client
Mas Romaní

Art Director
Gabriel Morales

Designer
Gabriel Morales

Year Produced
2007

Description
This is the wine label design for Mas Romaní.

Hatch Design
San Francisco, USA

Title
Charles Chocolates Packaging

Client
Charles Chocolates

Art Director
Joel Templin

Designer
Eszter Clark

Year Produced
2005

Description
Charles Chocolates, a premium chocolatier, was entering the high-end confections market. With sophisticated style and a good serving of whimsy, Hatch Design successfully made this new chocolate stand out. The hand-drawn logo and series of patterns, combined with elegant photography, and approachable colours culminated in the brand helps reflecting the quality of the product and achieves tremendous visibility from day one.

R Design
London, UK

Title
Selfridges & Co Brand Packaging

Client
Selfridges & Co

Art Director
Dave Richmond

Designer
Dave Richmond

Year Produced
2004

Description
A re-branded food range that echoes the store's forward thinking and contemporary attitude towards retailing. Although there were over 100 own brand products within the store, it was somewhat unrecognisable and lacked of shelf presence. The new approach was to create a range that was unique and that did not follow any traditional sector cues. Colour coding everything in black would make an incredible statement with only types, which could reflect what is inside for example strawberry jam and therefore, pink types would appear. Typeface, trade gothic range left used across the whole range in one same point size has ensured clarity and uniformity.

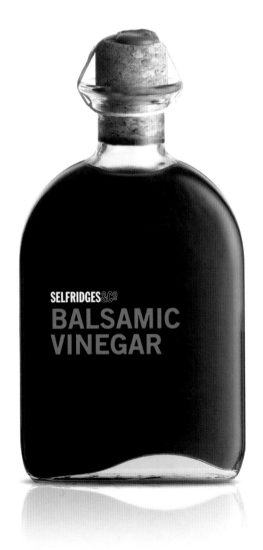

HP

QUINTA DE
S. VICENTE
Colheita Premium
AZEITE VIRGEM EXTRA

Herdeiros
Passanha
1738

0.50L
PORTUGAL

BaseDesign
Bruxelles, Belgium & New York, USA

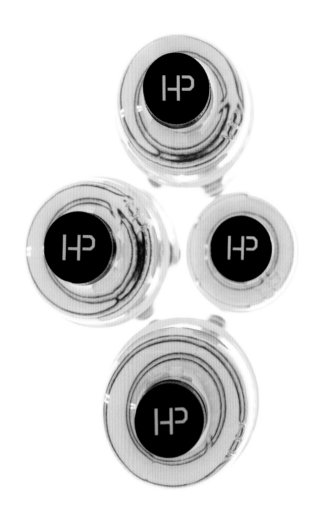

Title
Herdeiros Passanha Olive Oil

Client
Herdeiros Passanha

Art Director
BaseDesign

Designer
BaseDesign, Michael Young (Bottle design)

Year Produced
2008

Description
Herdeiros Passanha is a family-owned Portuguese company that until now has specialized in premium olive oil. Nearly carte blanche. The brief is set to re-brand the company, stressing on 'timeless elegance.'

To create a clear, coherent brand identity, the team brought in English industrial designer Michael Young to design the bottle. Created a simple icon – a rounded drop – to hint at the oil and its generous flavour. Paired this with a stencil typeface to convey all information, and yield a monogrammed bottle cap. Art direction and colour palette plays off the natural ingredients. Deliverables included three sizes of bottles, all communications materials, and a film, made by Base Motion, about the company and its fazenda.

The family is so pleased with the re-branding that they have decided to expand into vinegar, salt, sardines, aromatized oils, dried herbs, and skin care oils/soaps, for which Base will also do the branding.

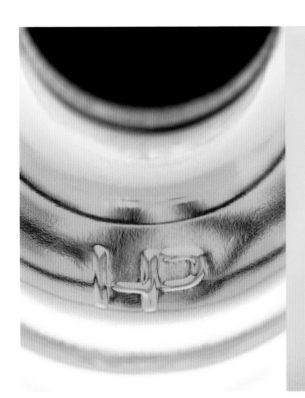

Slingshot Inc.
Toronto, Canada

Title
Food packaging

Client
Heavenly Sweets

Art Director
Ava Abbott

Designer
Melanie Marler

Year Produced
2008

Description
The love for the finer things in life inspired the exquisite line of cookies and chocolates. The packaging solution evokes the pure love of giving and the pleasure of receiving all while recalling the finer pastry shops of Europe and times gone by.

Mibo Ltd

East Sussex, UK

Title
Nudo Packaging

Client
Nudo Ltd

Art Director
Madeleine Rogers

Designer
Madeleine Rogers

Year Produced
2007

Description
The brief for Nudo's brand identity and olive oil tin was 'sophisticated but artisanal,' something that looked friendly but businesslike. For the logo, the client wanted something with stylishly handwritten types, so Mibo designed bespoke lettering and then added two delicate leaves hovering over the final letter, to make a direct connection between the company and the natural world it trades in. The repeating olive design has actually created as much of a brand identity as the logo itself, and these repeating motifs have subsequently been applied to all Nudo's products.

biz-R
Devon, UK

Title
Clive's' Rebranding & Packaging

Client
Clive's

Art Director
Blair Thomson

Designer
Blair Thomson, Tish England

Year Produced
2006

Description
To rebrand Buckfast Organic Bakery, Clive's and its range of products in order to communicate the passion and vibrancy of the company and it's unique range of handmade organic, vegetarian and gluten free products.

The logo combines a hand-drawn typeface with clean modern type to communicate the forward thinking values of the company together with the homemade qualities of the products.

The strapline 'made with love' emphasises the handmade healthy, organic products.

Handwritten comments and hand-drawn illustrations add humour and personality to the brand and give each product a sense of individuality.

Distinctive large typography, bright colours and bold photography focusing on the fresh organic ingredients, make the brand now easily identifiable and give it a contemporary confident appearance which will appeal to a much wider target audience.

biz-R
Devon, UK

Title
Clive's Pot Of

Client
Clive's'

Art Director
Blair Thomson

Designer
Blair Thomson

Illustrator
Paul Warren

Copywriter
Tish England

Year Produced
2008

Description
To challenge the existing packaging design in the market, currently saturated with uninspiring international brands and bland own label products, and through distinct differentiation, to assist Clive's as they expand and diversify their product range.

The sleeve format was adapted to maximise visibility of the product. biz-R printed on the reverse, matt side of the board to achieve a textured finish. Bold use of typography with symbology, pattern and colour from each recipe's origin creates a bold highly graphic identity.

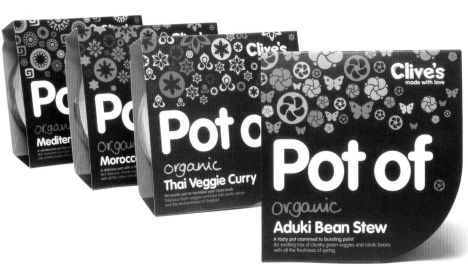

The Creative
Method
Sydney, Australia

Title
Over The Moon Brand Identity

Client
Over The Moon Dairy Co.

Art Director
Tony Ibbotson

Designer
Andi Yanto

Year Produced
2008

Description
The idea was to create a brand from scratch
that had immediate personality and character. A hand-crafted nature needed to be
conveyed whilst also operating in a premium
section of the market.

The myth that the moon is made of cheese
and the children's nursery rhyme 'Hey
Diddle Diddle' was the inspiration behind
the name. There was also a nice link with the
cows that produce the cheese who are unusu-
ally active in jumping around the paddock in
the early evenings.

The approach was to reflect a handmade but
premium quality so numerous sketches of
the letters were created until the final logo
was realized.

Stockholm
Design Lab
Stockholm, Sweden

Title	**Description**
IKEA FOOD Design and Packaging Concept	Stockholm Design Lab created a design and packaging concept for IKEA when the company combined its various food and catering units under the joint name IKEA FOOD. The packaging concept is for a range of food products sold under the IKEA FOOD label, expressing the key values: reliable, good quality and Swedish. The package design is based on three approaches – photographic, graphic and transparent.
Client	
IKEA	
Designer	
Stockholm Design Lab	
Year Produced	
2004 Ongoing	

MJÖLKCHOKLAD / Milk chocolate / Milchschokolade /
Chocolat au lait / Chocolate con leche / Chocolate
de leite / Melkchocolade / Melkchocolade / Σοκολάτα
ρόφημα / Cioccolato al latte / Maitosuklaa

IKEA® FOOD

LINGONMOUSSE

IKEA® FOOD   300 g

GRAVLAXSÅS

IKEA® FOOD   200 g

PEPPARROTSSÅS

IKEA® FOOD   200 g

GRAVAD LAX

IKEA® FOOD

200 g

LINGONSYLT

IKEA® FOOD   400 g

GRÄSLÖKS-
SÅS

IKEA® FOOD

HAVREFLARN / Sweet Oat Crisps / Hafertaler® / Galettes Suédoises
à l'Avoine / Ovsené Lupienky / Zabos sütemény / Kauralastuja /
Galletas de Avena / Bolachas de Aveia / Tallero all'Avena / Τραγανά
μπισκότα με βρώμη / Haverdaalders / Ciastka owsiane / Ovesné
Křupky / Овсяное хрустящее печенье / 燕麦脆干

Mayuko Hari
New York, USA

Title
COOKÜRU

Client
School Project

Art Director
Mayuko Hari

Designer
Mayuko Hari

Year Produced
2007

Description
This is a kitchen tool brand 'COOKÜRU (cooking and guru).' The packaging in uni-sex colour combination of black and salmon pink, shape, and graphics concentrates board target customers that can be men and women.

Products include utensils, British tea pot, and espresso maker.

contributors
contribuyentes
medewerkers
簡介
コントリビューター
기부자

cally, physically and commercially. The company collaborates naturally; they'll lead, steer and inspire, but also listen. This ability helps to create many long-term client relationships.
Page 074-075, 150-151

CHHUN TANG

The design duo of Chhun Tang and April Larivee is a mix of East meets West. Tang's clean, refined style mixed with Larivee's unrestrained creativity combines for a unique blend of work. Constantly evolving and growing, the ultimate goal of the pair is to use their skills in a positive way to help people.
Page 118-119

CODESIGN LTD

CoDesign Ltd was co-founded by Eddy Yu and Hung Lam in early 2003. The company specialises in branding and corporate identity, environmental graphics, literature and packaging design. Characterised by simple and effective design backed up by bold and innovative concepts, the work of CoDesign is trusted among major corporations and institutions in Hong Kong.
Page 016-019

DANIELLA DOMINGUES

Lives and works in São Paulo, Brazil, Domingues sees her work not only as a tool to solve visual problems, but rather a way to build up dialogues and to invite reflection.
Page 076

DANNY GOLDBERG DESIGN

A Tel Aviv-based studio specialises in boutique branding and art book design, it was founded in 2000 by Danny Goldberg, who is an award winning designer, a graduate with honour and a lecturer at the Bezalel Academy of Art and Design, Jerusalem. Among his prizes are the Ministry of Culture prize followed by an exhibition at the Israel Museum. In 2005, his works were appraised by the Japanese Design Foundation and exhibited in Osaka and Tokyo, and in 2005 and 2007 appeared in the annual publication of the Tokyo Type Directors Club. In 2007, Danny Goldberg Design opened its new office in Paris, France.
Page 188-189

DAVID BARATH DESIGN AND VISUAL GROUP BUDAPEST

Born and raised in Novi Sad in 1977, David Barath has been living in Budapest since 1993. After working several years for advertising agencies as graphic designer and art director, he followed his passion for photography and became creative producer of publishing house Marquard Media.

In the last seven years, Barath has outlined and produced several fashion and celebrity stories for various glossy magazines, while founding his own agency Visual Group. The agency continues its activity as 'a company for creative problem solv-

ing,' with Barath as the creative director, he personally works mostly as brand building specialist and graphic designer. He is also a creative consultant of a product design management company PapaMama Kollektív AB, signage producing company 321, and contemporary art gallery G13.
Page 032-033

DESIGN SANGSANG

Graduated in Graphic Design Studies in Chosun University, South Korea in 2006, Wdaru has been a designer for Design Sangsang since 2006. He participated in several design exhibitions and design festivals in Japan, Korea, Italy and Germany.
Page 182-187

DESIGNWORKS

Established in 1991, DESIGNWORKS is a multi-disciplinary marketing communications and design group providing fully integrated creative services to the commercial, industrial and public sectors. Their collective vision embraces 'Strategic Creativity,' working with clients on collaborative projects designed to enhance brand awareness, market position, effective communication and market yield.

DESIGNWORKS offers a full creative service, encompassing a variety of communication disciplines. This, combined with their broad understanding of brand-positioned design, enhanced by creative application, has proven invaluable as an effective communication resource to their clients.
Page 180

DFRAILE

Dfraile is a studio which projects its activity onto a variety of areas within graphic design where priority is given to a direct concept, together with a great idea whenever possible. It was founded in 2000 by designer Eduardo del Fraile. Their work has received a Gold Laus Award and several Silver Laus Awards. It has been featured in D&AD Annual.
Page 054-055, 102-103, 168, 202-203, 215

DIMAQUINA

Dimaquina is a design collective based in Rio de Janeiro and London, founded by Daniel Neves, Antonio Pedro Rezende and Alex Nako in 2005. They create stories, platforms and environments, where brands can move with functionality, efficiency and poetry. In this playground of ideas, where art and technology come together, everything escapes from a plain result to a deep experience of many interconnections. It is in the network culture where they find their storytelling.
Page 174-175

DOWLING DESIGN & ART DIRECTION

Dowling Design & Art Direction is an independent graphic design studio specialising in the generation of ideas and intelligent solutions that explore the possibilities of creativity and craft. They work closely with clients to achieve solutions that

are appropriate and engaging. They deliver coherent design solutions that work effectively across a wide range of applications, from books, brochures, magazines and promotional literature, to packaging, signage, websites and corporate identity systems. The company encourages creative collaboration and can call upon a network of experienced copywriters, photographers and illustrators to ensure that every aspect of a client's problem is addressed with equal care and attention.
Page 136, 161

DRAFT CO., LTD

Established in Tokyo in 1978, DRAFT has gained 30 years of solid experience and has gained various local and international design awards.
Page 037

DUOIDO

Since October of 2004, duoido projected to work as a duet, two graphic designers. National clothing brands at the beginning and later international brands have been strong experiences to improve their professionalism and to insert the company into the market. They create brands, redesigned and elaborated image concepts, they generate products looking for that from the support they have something to say.

To listen, to analyze and soon to translate necessities are part of duoido's daily work. Suitable analysis, pertinent translation of concepts and a demanding production of pieces causes each product to have duoido's distinctive mark.
Page 012-013

ELISABETH SOÓS

Elisabeth Soós graduated from the FH Joanneum Graz in 2006, and did her senior theses at BMW Designworks USA, California. She designed two Racing Cars for the TU Graz Formula Student, worked as an industrial designer at Pilotfish Munich, and did freelance projects for various companies, like Propeller Design and Cliff Design in Gothenburg, Sweden. Soós is living both in Austria and Germany now and going to run her own business – Soós Limited Design.
Page 105

ESPLUGA+ASSOCIATES

A strange company that works, since 1993, between advertising, naming, graphic design, branding and lots of things. It is not just a graphic design studio. They don't want to be an advertising agency. The truth is, it is quite difficult to define the company, but they do know what they really love: communication.
Page 020, 212-213

FORMAFANTASMA

FormaFantasma is a small and an intimate laboratory where took in place, experiment over different themes and media from illustrations to product, art and graphic design. All works are characterised by a personal way to express concept

and ideas, choosing to create 'only for themselves.' Forma-Fantasma is composed by Simone Farresin and Andrea Trimarchi, two young Italian designers and artists.
Page 014-015

H55
Hanson Ho, an award winning design director, founded his studio H55 in 1999. He has represented Singapore to create visual identities and design applications at the Venice Biennale International Art Exhibition 2005 and 2006, the recent Milan International Furniture Fair 2008, and the upcoming ICSID & IFI Design Conferences in 2009. Ho has received recognition and awards from some of the most prestigious international design competitions. He has also given lectures and workshops in design institutions, and was part of the design judging panel for the Singapore Creative Circle Awards 2006 and 2007, and the Crowbar Awards 2008.

His Rabbit project are currently on sale at the world-renowned Dover Street Market by Comme des Garçons in London, amongst other design stores around the world.
Page 198-199

HATCH DESIGN
Hatch Design is a firm based on the belief that the best design is honest, hands-on and human. Co-founded by Joel Templin and Katie Jain, Hatch Design helps new products and business get off the ground, and helps existing brands soar. Since opening their doors in the Spring of 2007, Hatch has created work for many renowned brands.
Page 205, 219

HAWAII
Hawaii was established in 2005 by Paul McAnelly. Based in London, the studio offers a diverse range of skills including design, illustration and art direction. The studio prides itself on creating unique, original work from concept to print.
Page 079

HELP REMEDIES
Help Remedies was created to make solving simple health issues easy by looking for the best solution. By stripping away some of the complexity and fear mongering of the health industry, they hope to make the category friendlier and more accessible, and in doing so to empowering people to make their own health decisions. It is believed that a little help, honesty and kindness would go for a long way.
Page 122-123

HOMEWORK
Homework is an independent graphic design studio and consultancy that focuses on art direction, visual identity and communication for lifestyle, fashion and cultural clients. Homework was established in 2002 by Jack Dahl. Dahl was responsible for kickstarting a visual presence and direction for international mens fashion publication HE magazine

and Cover magazine (Copenhagen). Among others, Dahl has worked with Self Service magazine and Work in Progress advertising design studio in Paris on some of today's leading fashion references including Jil Sander, Prada, Pucci, Chloé, Celine, Colette and Virgin Records.
Page 107, 196-197

HÖRÐUR LÁRUSSON
Hörður Lárusson is a graphic designer who was born and is working in Reykjavík, Iceland. He works at a studio and does a lot of freelance projects. When he is not working, he usually stays at home arranging his books by colours or does some cooking, enjoying his life.
Page 077

ICO DESIGN CONSULTANCY LIMITED
ico is a small, sociable and prolific design team with a successful 12-year history. In the central London studio, ico creates brands and produces exceptional print and digital media pieces for clients from the arts, property, leisure, interior design and museum sector.

ico likes to say that they have no style. Every single project on its site is a result of listening to their clients, understanding the brief and suggesting solutions that engage with the target audience. It might sound simple, but it's the basis of their business.
Page 046-047

IMAGEFED
Imagefed is driven by Washington DC-based creative, Matthew Curry, it is a Grammy Nominated® studio specialising in various creative disciplines including music packaging, branding, motion, conceptual, character design, editorial illustration, interactive applications and events.
Page 060-061

INCORPORATED CREATIVE UNIT
Born in 1978, Bai Gang Gang graduated from Xi'an Fine Arts Academy. He started working for Ogilvy & Mather as art director in 2002 and later became an independent designer in 2004. In 2005, Bai co-founded an independent music label Vowelmusic. In 2007, he co-founded a design studio Incorporated Creative Unit.
Page 067

JAMIE WIECK
He is a graphic designer and illustrator based in London. He likes to solve problems.
Page 166-167

JESSE KIRSCH
Jesse Kirsch is an award-winning graphic designer with a passion for typography, minimalism, packaging, and working in 3-dimensions. After honing his skills at New York's School of

Visual Arts, Kirsch went on to design for clients like Atlantic Records and Columbia University. He currently lives and works at home in Edison, New Jersey.
Page 112-113, 137, 208

JOYN:VISCOM
Wei Xingyu is a graphic designer, an illustrator, and is the partner of JOYN:VISCOM studio. He is now working and living in Beijing, focusing on iconograph, typeface design, toys, street art and other media based upon different kinds of iconograph. Specialising in Chinese graffiti typeface design, he cooperates with a lot of big names like Nike, Motorola, Converse, etc.
Page 149

JULIA HOFFMANN
Julia Hoffmann currently is the creative director of Advertising and Graphic Design at the Museum of Modern Art in New York. Prior to that, she worked as the art director at the ado-based agency Crispin Porter + Bogusky, where she worked for clients such as Burger King, Nike, and Microsoft, as well as leading the Volkswagen account.

She had previously worked with the New York design firm Pentagram, where she designed identities and branding systems, packaging, and publication designs. She also developed the redesign of The Metropolitan Opera in New York, and was the lead designer on the award-winning bestselling book The Daily Show with Jon Stewart Presents America: A Citizen's Guide to Democracy Inaction.
Page 051

JUNGESCHACHTEL
The Berlin-based design agency jungeschachtel was founded in 2006 by Nina Dautzenberg and Andrea Gadesmann. They have known each other since their childhood and they became graphic and product designers in Berlin and Amsterdam after their studies in Paris, New York and London.
Page 158-159

KINETIC
Established as an interactive design agency in 1999, Kinetic is a part of the Ad Planet Group, the largest locally owned advertising company in Singapore.

The team has been winning various local and international awards, from the Singapore Creative Circle Awards (CCA) to the One Show in New York. In 2001, Kinetic was the only interactive agency in the world to bag two Gold awards at the One Show. Adding a Design and Advertising arm in 2001 for more firepower, creating an integrated creative shop, the agency apparently continued to garner a good share of clients and awards. In 2004, Kinetic was placed the third at the CCA, and was the top performing Asian agency at the One Show 2005.
Page 110-111, 148

KNOEND LLC
Knoend LLC is an ecodesign company dedicated to bringing accessible, affordable, environmentally friendly products to consumer markets. By using materials that are biodegradable, recycled or recyclable, salvaged or reusable, Knoend's designs will lessen landfill waste. Knoend's goal is to change the consumer product culture in a proactive way that will reduce manufacturing and shipping waste and provide sustainable solutions that extend the traditional dead-end product lifecycle.
Page 134

LITTLE FURY
Little Fury is the design collaborative of Esther Mun and Tina Chang. The two girls met at Pentagram in New York. Later, they quit their jobs and founded their design studio Little Fury and set to work designing their first product line.
Page 171

MARQUE
Marque is a branding consultancy with a contemporary view of the world. They work collectively across three studios in London, New York, Glasgow respectively. Their specialisations are position, identity and communication where they bring energy, dedication and sensitivity.
Page 192-193

MASH
As a graphic design studio, Mash takes a few well-chosen designers, brand creators, simplifiers and solutionists with a passion for what it does. Putting in the awkward position of having to define themselves, and feeling a little like they are putting an ad in the singles column, Mash is a studio that caters specially to clients who truly want to build their brand with creativity and originality.
Page 216

MAXIME DELPORTE
Maxime Delporte is a French graphic designer living in Brussels. He enjoys testing on various pure graphics, typography and doing research of any kind of installations.
Page 128-129

MAYUKO HARI
Born in Tokyo, Japan, Mayuko is a degree holder of Bachelor of Fine Arts in Packaging Design and Associate of Science in Fine Arts in Display and Exhibit Design.
Page 232

MEGAN CUMMINS
Graduated in Graphic Design and Photography in Savannah College of Art & Design, Cummins believes that materials can say just as much as the actual graphics on a product. A package should be so captivating and delicious that users cannot resist picking it up and live without it. The satisfaction

of creating this experience is what drives her to make graphic design as her passion as well as profession.
Page 190-191

MIBO LTD
Madeleine Rogers launched Mibo in 2001 with a range of boldly-patterned lampshades, which were an immediate commercial success.

Since then, she has divided her time between continuing to design products for Mibo's in-house homewares and designing for a diverse range of clients. Surface pattern is a key to her work and her clear-crisp style has always been instantly recognisable.
Page 225

MICHAEL YOUNG LTD
Michael Young has been amongst the most successful and influential designers of his generation from the outset of his career in 1992. In 1995, he created his first design office in London, and from then on he's been focusing on a series of projects for Cappellini, Sawaya & Moroni and Magis, to name a few.

Young is currently based in Hong Kong, where he enjoys direct access to factories in China. He hopes that, by bringing the design closer to those production facilities he will be able to elevate the awareness and appreciation for the art of design in that key market.
Page 154-157, 170

MOMENT DESIGN STUDIO
Born in Northeast China, Xiaoxue is currently living and working in Beijing. He established MOMENT design studio in 2005 and now working for a music magazine and in the fashion industry. Movies, his childhood memory in 70s, fantastic dramas, universe, future, music and some others often inspired him in creations.
Page 146-147

NAOTO FUKASAWA
Born in Japan in 1956, Naoto Fukasawa graduated from Tama Art University's Product Design Department, Tokyo, in 1980. Since 2001, he was an advisor for MUJI, involving in the design direction of household goods. In 2003, he established Naoto Fukasawa Design in Tokyo. He later launched Plus Minus Zero, a new brand of electronic household appliances and sundries. He has designed for companies in Italy, Germany, Switzerland and Northern Europe and also for major electronic industries in Japan.
Page 169

NIKKI FARQUHARSON
Nikki Farquharson is currently studying for a degree in Graphic and Media Design at the London College of Communication. When Farquharson designs, she wants to com-

municate the message with simplicity, whether it'd be with typography or imagery. Farquharson believes that it allows her to become more accessible to a wider audience. Illustrating gives her the freedom to express herself as an individual so it tends to be ornate and abstract. Her goal is to find herself in a position that will allow her to merge her design ideas and illustration in order to create something new.
Page 152-153

NIPPON DESIGN CENTER, INC.
Born in 1958, Kenya Hara is a graphic designer, a representative in Nippon Design Center, Inc. and a professor in Musashino Art University. In 2001, Hara was enlisted as an advisory board member for MUJI, and since then has art-directed planning and advertising to espouse MUJI's new vision.

Concentrating on identification and communication, Hara has made his expertise the design not of 'things that are,' but of 'things that happen.' He has been awarded in various fields and encompassing diverse activities, including advertising, signage, book design and identification.
Page 209-211

NONAME NOSHOP
A Seoul-based independent design studio consists of 6 members including Kim Geun-tae, Kim Jong-buhm, Lee Shin-hye, Lee Hye-yeon, Chun Ji-hyang and Park Kyung-oak. The studio was established in 2003 to give names to things that have 'no name' and to make products with things and ideas that 'no shop' considered. NONAME NOSHOP has been working across a wide range of disciplines including graphics, exhibition planning, space design, and product design.
Page 072-073, 126-127, 130-133

NON-FORMAT
Non-Format is based in London, UK and Minneapolis, USA, it is a creative team comprising a Norwegian Kjell Ekhorn and a British Jon Forss. They work on a range of projects including art direction, design and illustrations for music industry, arts and culture, fashion and advertising clients. They also art direct Varoom, the journal of illustration and images.
Page 142-143

ODD
ODD is an independent creative and design agency based in London, UK.
Page 080-081

OMD CONTEMPORARY DESIGN TERMINAL
Li Degeng and Jiang Hua established OMD Contemporary Design Terminal Ltd in 2008, it is a creative team with high innovation spirit and is based on multidiscipline. It provides a comprehensive platform for curation, publication, designing and research. It tries all means to explore more social energy for current designing. Thus

initiatively OMD involves itself in many social production scopes, intending to give full rein to designing in every new field and node, meanwhile exploring the meaning of design.

OMD claims to be the collaborator of social production, standing aloof from the traditional handicraft model. Meanwhile OMD is also the creator and explorer of contemporary aesthetics of new design. As an open platform and network, OMD covers unlimited cooperative fields. Now it has companions from various fields like designing, writing, research, curation, critics, arts and music, etc.

PEARLFISHER
Founded in London in 1992, Pearlfisher is a leading independent design agency owned and managed by three partners who opened their second studio in 2003 in New York. They cooperate with the biggest international clients from South Africa, Asia, America and Western Europe.

Pearlfisher creates future desire for brands, their philosophy is based on the concept of truth and desire: 'uncovering the essential truth at the heart of a brand and expressing it in a way that consumers will find desirable as they move into the future.' Pearlfisher needs a clear perspective on the future to identify the cultural shifts that will impact consumer behaviour, and approaches every project with an awareness of its potential future impact on the environment.

PURPOSE LTD
Purpose is a graphic design consultancy committed to producing design that promotes clarity and creates design that helps people to communicate more effectively. Purpose creates visual identities, print, exhibition and pack designs for a variety of clients, from individuals to global organisations.

R DESIGN
David Richmond first formed a company called David Richmond Associates in 1991 on his kitchen table. He had no clients and no associates but he had a vision and a passion for branding and packaging design. As their reputation with the number of clients and employees grew, he changed the name to R Design. From its conception, the company still remains their guiding principles 'Be sharp, clear and creative.'

17 years on, Richmond likes to think they make companies and their products look good and make brands feel and act better. They create character where there is none. R Design sells confidence and has helped all their clients behave like leaders.

RYSZARD BIENERT
Born in 1976, Ryszard Bienert graduated in 2002 from Academy of Fine Arts In Poznan, Poland. After 7 years working as an art director in a few advertising agencies, Bienert is now working as a freelancer.

SAMURAI INC.
Born in Tokyo in 1965, Kashiwa Sato graduated from Tama Art University with a degree in graphic design in 1989. After working for Hakuhodo Inc., Japan's second largest advertising agency, Sato established 'SAMURAI' creative studio in 2000 and is the art director and the creative director of the studio. He received many prizes such as Mainichi Design Award, Tokyo ADC Grand Prix, Asahi Advertising Award, Kamekura Yusaku Award and Japan Package Design Award Gold Medal. His expanding visions and creative works in various fields is highly acclaimed.

SANTOS&KARLOVICH™
Santos&Karlovich™ is a multimedia, experimental, design studio based in New York City, founded Virgilio Santos and Nedjelco-Michel Karlovich who both met while working as designers at ATTIK. Within the last year, they'd gathered all of work that they had done together experimentally and formed their own studio.

SARAH CIHAT
Sarah Cihat was born and raised in Tennessee. She studied fashion design before going to London for a semester abroad, then returned to the States to pursue a degree in Product Design at Parsons School of Design. Since then, her work has been featured in many publications as well as in exhibitions such as the St. Etienne International Design Biennial and Salone di Mobile. She enjoys the hands-on quality of product design and has a great appreciation for hand-crafted objects and antiques. She strives to create unpretentious, to invite designs that transcend trends and are ecologically responsible. She is now working in her studio in Brooklyn, USA.

SEA
Established in 1997 by Bryan Edmondson and John Simpson, SEA is an independent, multi-disciplinary and award-winning design agency based in London, UK.

SEED CREATIVE CONSULTANTS
SEED is an independently owned and creatively driven consultancy founded in London, UK. It provides product-based marketing solutions and revolutionary packaging ideas. SEED believes that regardless of what form these ideas take, they must be beautifully crafted, intelligently simple and most important of all human – if they are to be meaningful

to their audience. This deep-rooted philosophy has attracted companies for whom craftsmanship and innovation lie at the very heart of their philosophy. They include Mercedes-Benz, Volvo, Chanel, Porsche Design and Shiseido amongst others.

SHYA-LA-LA PRODUCTION LIMITED
Shya-La-La is an independent visual communications agency that understands the important relationship between companies and their target customers. With a team of enthusiastic individuals experienced in various disciplines, the agency offers a one-stop integrated communication with a 'soul.'

From visual design to advertising, product design to packaging, corporate identity to collaterals, photography to multimedia, character design to illustration and content licensing, Shya-La-La believes that projects with a wholesome concept that is artistically presented will have a lasting impression in consumers' mind. Their objective is to create a bridge through the marketing process, and their vision is to speak to clients' consumers via their creations. The agency believes there is nothing that cannot be done.

SLINGSHOT INC.
Slingshot are brand builders. As a multidisciplinary team established in 1999, they deliver focused brand visual communication strategies. Whether defining a brand or refining an existing strategy, their belief remains: Branding builds demand, Slingshot creates that demand.

SMALL
Small offer creative and strategic art direction for identity, literature packaging and exhibitions. Small has a reputation for working for quintessentially 'English' brands such as Anglepoise®, fashion designer Margaret Howell and Saville Row tailors Gieve and Hawkes, architects Foster & Partners, furniture and lifestyle store Heals, Product designer Alexander Taylor, D&AD and BAFTA.

Small. Because you don't need to be big to be clever.

SON OF TAM
Son of Tam (Jason Tam) is a Hong Kong born, New York based designer. Growing up with Transformers, Power Rangers, and Flintstones vitamin chews, he aims to create work that brings out the part of himself that cannot be defined with a particular medium, language, or style. He is working his way towards his own personal renaissance.

STILETTO NYC
Stiletto nyc is a design studio based in New York and Milan, that specialises in art direction and design for print and video.

Co-founded in 2000 by Stefanie Barth and Julie Hirschfeld, the studio takes on projects spanning motion graphics, print and environmental design for international clients, such as the New York Times, Nike, HBO and several artists and boutiques in Europe and America, among others.

The studio has been featured in various international publications and has won two art director awards for their motion graphics. In 2006, Stiletto was invited to speak at Semipermanent Design conference in Sydney, Australia and the studio is also featured in Area 2 -The international guide to contemporary graphics by Phaidon Press in 2008. Their work will be on display in BRNO (CZ) at the 23. International Biennial of Graphic Design.
Page 038

STOCKHOLM DESIGN LAB
Based in Stockholm, Sweden, Stockholm Design Lab also works internationally. Nevertheless, their Scandinavian origins help to create relevant, functional solutions that reflect and influence the society and times the team lives in.

The Laboratory has been working on the entire corporate identities of companies and institutions for 10 years. Their clients have tended to regard identity as a total experience rather than a matter of positioning the logo on the surface.

Design is assumed to be their starting-point, but in Scandinavia, the team is alone in defying all attempts at disciplinary restrictions. Thanks to this cross-border philosophy, the team created a brand for themselves.
Page 090-098, 106, 230-231

STUDIO COPYRIGHT
Studio Copyright is a young design team from different areas that wants to offer different creative services, based in investigation and innovation on communicative languages. The studio has gained solid experience on brand services, publishing, promotional design, multimedia, motion graphics and typography.
Page 218

STUDIO KANNA
Akiko Kanna moved to England in 1995, and graduated from Central Saint Martins College of Art & Design of BA Graphic Design. Experienced working at Dazed & Confused in London while she was a student, after graduated from the collage, Kanna was employed by a design company North based in London for 4 years and has gained many opportunities in design field in the UK. Kanna returned to Japan in 2006 and set up her own studio. Keeping the same design attitude towards any projects, Kanna is always open-minded and welcomes any design approach.
Page 124-125

THE CREATIVE METHOD
The Creative Method is a multi-disciplined, award-winning design agency that has a broad spectrum of clients, ranging from small family businesses to large multi-nationals. It was formed in October 2005 with the sole purpose of creating world-class design work. They have a focus on 'new-to-world' brand creation with a strong consumer bias.

Based on their inception, the agency has created new brand solutions for clients from the UK, Germany, USA, Singapore, Philippines, Vietnam, Australia and New Zealand.
Page 200-201, 228-229

THE PARTNERS
Formed in 1983, The Partners delivers brand strategy and design for clients who require outstandingly creative solutions. The most awarded creative agency in the UK, The Partners is also recognised by peers within the group as WPP's most creative agency.

With 25 years experience of producing new brands, rejuvenating existing brands and consulting across all areas of visual strategy, The Partners has a wide range of expertise which spans many sectors and includes working with some of the world's most notable brands including Deloitte, Ford, Jaguar, McKinsey & Company, Hilton and Davidoff, as well as producing creative benchmark work for the likes of The National Gallery, BBC, Wedgwood and Wolf Theiss.
Page 217

THORBJØRN ANKERSTJERNE
Thorbjørn Ankerstjerne is from Copenhagen, Denmark. He lives and works in London where he just graduated from Central Saint Martins, with a BA (Hons) in Graphic Design. He loves to combine and experiment with different techniques and materials to solve a brief, and sees every project as a new opportunity and challenge to explore innovative ways of communicating.
Page 026-027, 044-045, 053

TOM DIXON
In the early 1980s, Tom Dixon learnt to weld and as a result invented a career as a radical designer in innovative furniture. His career path has since roller coasted through luxury goods, working with labels such as Cappellini and Swarovski, picking up medals along the way such as the Order of the British Empire in 2000. He is also involved with high street giant Habitat, where he is the creative director. Dixon continues to innovate through the iconic modernist company Artek and his own label, snappily named 'Tom Dixon.'
Page 140-141

TURNER DUCKWORTH
Since setting up in 1992, Turner Duckworth have stayed true to their passion for designing consumer brand identities and packaging that generate commercial results and creative awards. The two studios in London and San Francisco col-

laborate on every project. Work flows freely between each to give clients a rich and nuanced perspective from both sides of the Atlantic.

They conduct distant crits on all the projects, in which each studio critiques the other's work with no punches pulled. The result is a well-informed and objective view that produces exceptional clarity for their consumers' brands.
Page 099

UNDOBOY
Undoboy's design embraces with a simple philosophy 'design brings happiness' and the works include brand identity design, editorial design, interactive design, character design, packaging design, toy design, motion graphics, and illustration.
Page 084-085

WALDO PANCAKE
Jim Smith is an illustrator, designer and copywriter specialising in humorous, comic approaches.
Page 172-173

WHY NOT ASSOCIATES
Why Not Associates is a London based design company founded in 1987 which specialises in finding new and innovative communication solutions via a range of media including print, moving image and public art. The company is celebrated for combining a commercial responsibility with a passion for experimentation and innovation. This has lead to a range of successful projects for an impressive list of clients.
Page 024-025

WILLIAMS MURRAY HAMM
Established in 1997, Williams Murray Hamm offers clients alternatives to the intrusive logos and graphic formulas that had become common in the 1980's and 1990's. WMH quickly gained an international reputation for creative and commercial success winning major awards at D&AD, Design Week, Clio, New York Festivals, Mobius, Type Directors, and Communication Arts. In the UK, the business is best known for its 2002 DBA Grand Prix winner Hovis. Twice winning Agency of the Year, the business was ranked No. 1 for design effectiveness in 2003, 2004 and 2006 and No1 for creativity in 2005, 2006 and 2007.
Page 204

ZNP CREATIVE CO., LTD
Zinoo Park is a designer who uses both products and graphics to express his design concept, that is well paced with the pop culture. He knows which elements excite the public and uses them to highlight issues within the society. During his 2-year experience at The Royal College of Art, Park endeavors to become more engaged with pop culture.
Page 104

Acknowledgement

We would like to thank all the designers and companies who made
significant contribution to the compilation of this book. Without them,
this project would not be able to accomplished. We would also like
to thank all the producers for their invaluable assistance throughout this
entire proposal. The successful completion also owes a great deal to many
professionals in the creative industry who have given us precious insights
and comments. We are also very grateful to many other people whose
names did not appear on the credits but have made specific input and
continuous support the whole time.

Viction:ary

Future Editions

If you would like to contribute to the next edition of Victionary, please
email us your details to submit@victionary.com